Perso
Unlin

CW01497220

Dean Atta is an award-winning author and performance poet. He won the 2012 London Poetry Award and was named as one of the most influential LGBT people by the *Independent on Sunday* Pink List. He has written two YA novels-in-verse, including *The Black Flamingo* which was a top-selling debut of 2020, and was shortlisted for the Waterstones Children's Book Prize, CILIP Carnegie Medal, the Jhalak Prize and the YA Book Prize. *The Black Flamingo* was also awarded the prestigious Stonewall Book Award and the Carnegie Shadowers' Choice Award 2020. *Person Unlimited* is his non-fiction debut.

@DeanAtta

Praise for Dean Atta

'He follows no trend; he seeks no favours . . . Beyond black, beyond white, beyond straight, beyond gay, so I say'
BENJAMIN ZEPHANIAH

'Dean Atta is man on a mission'
TOM ROBINSON, BBC 6 Music

'The Gil Scott Heron of his generation'
CHARLIE DARK

'I can do nothing but take my hat off to Dean Atta for speaking out, saying what he believed, and doing it so effectively and powerfully that countless people heard it who would never normally have done so'
Huffington Post

Also by Dean Atta

Poetry
I Am Nobody's Nigger
There is (still) love here

For young adults
The Black Flamingo
Only on the Weekends
I Can't Even Think Straight

For children
Confetti

Person Unlimited

An Ode to My Black Queer Body

Dean Atta

CANONGATE

This paperback edition published in Great Britain in 2025
by Canongate Books

First published in Great Britain in 2024
by Canongate Books Ltd, 14 High Street, Edinburgh EH1 1TE

canongate.co.uk

1

Extract from *Checking Out Me History* by John Agard.
Copyright © 1996. Reproduced by kind permission of John Agard
c/o Caroline Sheldon Literary Agency Ltd.

Extract from *I Am Nobody's Nigger* by Dean Atta.
Copyright © 2013. Published by Westbourne Publishers Ltd.
Reproduced with permission of the Licensor through PLSclear.

British Library Cataloguing-in-Publication Data
A catalogue record for this book is available on
request from the British Library

ISBN 978 1 83885 568 0

Typeset in Sabon by Palimpsest Book Production Ltd,
Falkirk, Stirlingshire

Printed and bound by CPI Group (UK) Ltd, Croydon CR0 4YY

The manufacturer's authorised representative in the EU for product
safety is Authorised Rep Compliance Ltd, 71 Lower Baggot Street,
Dublin D02 P593 Ireland (arccompliance.com)

For Mummy

Contents

HEART

LEFT HAND

BELLY

ROOTS

An Ode to My Black Queer Body

You've fought and you've run away. You've danced with other Black queer bodies until sunrise. You've stumbled into saunas and been touched by hands with faces you don't remember. You've grown an afro that strangers touched without permission. You've grown dreadlocks and received special greetings from Rastafarians. When you grew your beard, strangers regarded you with even greater suspicion. You were asked if you were Muslim, and a colleague joked that you looked like a terrorist. You let a man masturbate you in the water as your family sunbathed on the beach unawares. You've done so much in secret, in parks and graveyards, in parked cars and moving trains, in toilets, in stairwells and garages. Sometimes you wanted to be caught and sometimes you wanted to be held. You've had many sexually transmitted infections. You've taken PEP and PrEP so that you wouldn't get the one that many fear. You've been afraid of so many things but mostly your own mind. Sometimes you think of stepping into traffic or jumping off a bridge. You've taken drugs for fun and to feel numb. You've been sober. You've been vegan and not vegan and vegan again. You've meditated for many hours, sometimes for ten minutes a day and sometimes for ten days at a time on a silent retreat. You've retreated from your life in many ways. Sometimes depression has kept you from the world. Sometimes grief. You've kissed your grandfather's forehead after he was dead. You've held your nieces up to the sky to make them fly. You've given yourself wings. You've created an alter ego with a wig and heels. You've painted your face and nails. You've painted the walls of the home you live in with your boyfriend. You've looked at him with lust and with envy. In recent years, your waist size has gone up, your hairline has gone back and there are grey hairs in your beard. Your boyfriend looks at you like you are so sexy, but you know you are so much more. With all that you've endured, you are nothing less than miraculous.

CROWN

Good Hair

My first word was 'light', according to Mummy. She told me I said it as she, a teenage single parent, cradled me with one arm and paced around our bed and breakfast room. This wasn't a holiday B&B; it was where Mummy and I lived for the first year of my life, where Mummy pointed and named everything for me. 'Light' was the first word I learned to repeat. And, as Mummy repeated this story throughout my childhood, it became as real to me as any of my own memories.

This isn't a coming-of-age story. This isn't a coming-out story. This isn't a chronological story. This is a story of coming to terms with what I remember. Shining a light on the memories that make me the Black queer man I am today.

My mum and dad didn't marry. They split soon after I was born. I grew up with an abundance of other mixed-race boys around me. Mummy was friends with their mums. Did Mummy consciously surround me with other boys who looked like me, or was she unwittingly attracted to friendships with other white women with mixed-race children?

Mixed-race meant having a white mum and a Black dad. It meant having soft curly hair that people liked to touch and compliment. The concept of 'good hair' wasn't an idea I understood as a child.

I was born in northwest London in 1984. In the eighties and nineties, white women, including Mummy, would get curly perms to achieve the loose spiral curls that many mixed-race people had naturally growing from their scalps. If you search 'curly perm 1990s' online, you'll likely see photos of white Hollywood actresses with permed hair like mixed-race Mariah Carey's natural look.

I didn't know Mariah Carey was mixed-race until my teens. I'd assumed she was a white woman with a perm. Whitney Houston had a similar style in the video for her 1987 hit song 'I Wanna Dance with Somebody (Who Loves Me)'. My favourite song. I listened to it on cassette tape; it was the first song on side one of her debut album, *Whitney*. On the album cover she has a white vest top on, striking red lipstick framing a bright white smile and big hair in loose curls.

I was sure that if the coils of my hair were allowed to grow it would look like eighties Whitney or nineties Mariah. I was envious of one of the mixed-race boys from my primary school with long loose golden-brown curls to his shoulders, but he was often mistaken for a girl, and I didn't want that to happen to me.

Until the late fifteenth century, the word 'girl' was used for children of either sex, but in the sixteenth century people began to use 'girl' and 'boy' in opposition to each other. I was a boy of the twentieth century, but I was different to other boys. There wasn't a kind word available to refer to a boy like me. There was 'tomboy' for girls who wanted to wear dungarees and climb trees. But where was the equivalent word for a boy like me, a boy who wanted to wear dresses, a crown of daisies and play with Barbies?

I didn't wear dresses or a crown of flowers, but I did ask Mummy for a Barbie doll. I loved combing Barbie's straight blonde hair with her tiny pink plastic hairbrush. She was an object onto which I projected my frivolous fantasy of being a white woman with long blonde hair. I showed my Barbie to girls but hid her when boys came round to play. It was only my Barbie doll I hid from other boys. Other dolls were okay to have on display such as my troll dolls with multicoloured hair and squat bodies and my He-Man action figure with blond hair and six-pack abs.

Mummy took me to a Saturday stage school when I was four. I took singing, dance and drama classes for a few months, but I soon told Mummy I wanted to stay home on Saturdays and watch cartoons, play with my toys and video games.

Mummy took me to a glass-fronted northwest London barbershop full to bursting with Black men: customers and those there to accompany them and enjoy the social aspect of this space. It was a five-minute walk from my Cypriot grandparents' house. It was raucous, with Jamaican dance-hall, reggae, R&B and hip-hop blasting through the speakers and patois spoken between barbers and customers alike. I didn't understand much of it. My ears were open, but my eyes were fixed on the pixelated screen of my light grey Game Boy until it was my turn to sit in the barber's chair. He took off my glasses and set them aside, he wrapped me in a cape to cover my clothes and he cut my hair. The closest I came to wearing a dress as a boy was this barber's cape, the altar server cassocks and choir robes at church.

My Cypriot grandparents' house and this predominantly Jamaican barbershop situated in the same corner of north-west London gave me a sense of the worlds I was supposed to be part of. But speaking neither Cypriot Greek nor Jamaican patois made it hard to feel I belonged in either of them. I understood some Greek and some patois, but

I'd reply in a soft RP – received pronunciation – English accent.

One of my earliest memories of my Cypriot grandparents is Yiayia cutting Bapou's straight, dark brown hair in their garden. This garden holds my earliest memories of Yiayia and Bapou. Yiayia wears a bright floral summer dress and hangs laundry out to dry while Bapou tends to his roses. Yiayia hands me a cup of tea and a plate of biscuits or a plate of apple slices and orange segments. These are my formative memories of wordless acts of service. Yiayia and Bapou were silent more often than not, and silence felt safe to me.

I wanted to blend in at my Church of England primary school. I joined the school choir, and we appeared on the Christian TV show *Songs of Praise* in an episode filmed at the world-renowned boarding school, Eton College. There were no fees to pay to attend my primary school, but it felt exclusive in its own particular way. We got random opportunities like these: singing on *Songs of Praise*, going to ballets at the Royal Albert Hall, and modelling for a Dorling Kindersley book about the human body.

There's a blond boy on the front cover of the *Human Body* book in a front double bicep pose, a pose I'd also modelled for, but my photo hadn't made the cut. Inside the book, I stick my tongue out at the camera, fake sneeze into a red and white polka dot handkerchief and flex my prepubescent muscles in a back double bicep pose. Photo-ready: my short curls trimmed with scissors on top, cropped and faded with clippers on the back and sides. There's a double-page spread about types of hair in which a group of us are in a line-up with our backs to the camera. The text above our heads explains how, similar to skin, the amount of melanin in hair makes it dark or fair, and how different hair follicle shapes make different hair textures. There's nothing in there about the concept of 'good hair'. It wasn't until my twenties when I watched a documentary called *Good Hair* by Chris Rock and my thirties when I read a book called *Don't Touch My Hair* by Emma Dabiri that I began to understand how hair was tangled up in centuries of racism and misogyny; in what bell hooks called 'white-supremacist capitalist patriarchy', a system that privileges white, heterosexual and cisgender men. But I hadn't read bell hooks back then.

The most influential texts at my primary school were prayers and hymns, the prevailing rhetoric was 'What Would Jesus Do?', and the dress code was neat school uniform and neat hair. 'Neat' was implicitly understood to mean no lines or patterns shaved into your hair, which was a style most popular among Black and mixed-race boys. But in the school holidays, I was allowed lines and patterns, such as the Nike tick shaved into the back of my head.

Picture me: a seven-year-old boy branded from head to toe with the Nike logo. My hooded top, tracksuit bottoms and trainers were all Nike. I didn't know Nike was a winged goddess from Greek mythology and that what's commonly known as the Nike tick, or the Swoosh, represents the wings of this goddess of victory. And yet I felt a small flutter of victory when I reached for the back of my head to trace the tick.

This was the height of fashion to me. This small symbol made me feel good, made me feel cool. Mummy was cool for allowing me to make this choice. Whether it was what toys I played with, how I spent my Saturdays or how I had my hair cut, Mummy always afforded me choice.

Singed Hair

Little Sis's dad had dreadlocks, which I thought were cool. I was eight when Little Sis was born in 1992. I was envious that her dad was around at the beginning. Her dad is Jamaican, like mine.

Because Little Sis and I have the same mix and similar hair, we look alike, and it was rarely mentioned that we were half-siblings. Her dad is a music producer who had a UK number 1 hit in the nineties. He didn't live with us for long and soon we were a single-parent household again.

I asked to go back to Saturday stage school. I'd landed roles in several school plays and my talent for performance was affirmed and encouraged by schoolteachers and schoolmates alike. Their belief in me as a performer helped me to believe in myself.

At primary school most of my friends were girls (while the boys played football, the girls and I played cat's cradle, using our hands to make patterns from a forty-inch loop of string), and I was the only boy invited to their sleepovers. But at ten I had my first girlfriend, The Irish Dancer. I gave her a gold necklace with a little gold heart as a Valentine's Day gift. She accepted it and with it she accepted me as her boyfriend. She had an Indian dad and an Irish mum. She had light brown skin and chestnut brown hair down to her bum.

The previous year the smell of her singed hair had filled the C of E church like the incense of a Greek Orthodox church. She carried the crucifix, Christ on the cross wearing a crown of thorns, down the aisle in the direction of the stained-glass windows depicting another Jesus, and one of the candle bearers beside her set her hair on fire.

When The Irish Dancer and I sat on her bed with the door closed, I thought she was going to kiss me.

'I want to show you something,' she said, a quiver in her voice.

Was this something more than a kiss? Her breasts? Her vagina?

Mummy had given me a book with information about puberty and sex, with diagrams of the male and female anatomy. Even though The Irish Dancer was my girlfriend, and I knew about sex, I was ten, and I had no intentions of having sex with her.

She stood and walked over to her CD player and hit play. When the fiddle playing started, I had no idea what was happening. I was amazed and relieved, watching The Irish Dancer's frenetic footwork. Her straight arms glued to her sides, her stiff upper body, her straight brown hair and her pleated school uniform skirt bouncing up and down. I was amazed because I'd not seen anything like it besides *Riverdance* on TV and relieved because she wasn't going to kiss me or undress. This was her secret that no one at school knew about.

My secret was that I was gay. I thought The Irish Dancer was the most beautiful girl in my year, but I didn't want to kiss her. A few months later at a birthday party we were pressured into kissing by schoolmates. Our front teeth knocked together and everyone laughed. I was relieved when The Irish Dancer broke up with me, but Mummy wasn't best pleased.

'I can't believe I spent twenty pounds on a silly gold heart necklace for you to give to that girl,' she said.

Money made Mummy anxious. Many things made Mummy anxious.

Little Sis's hair made Mummy anxious. There was an abundance of it. Her fluffy afro was cute when she was one and two, but nursery school has judgemental parents at drop-off and pick-up time, tutting and shaking their heads.

'I don't want people to think I can't take care of them,' I overheard Mummy say on the house-phone. 'I have to learn to plait her hair.'

Unlike my barbershop haircuts, Little Sis's hair upkeep wasn't cheap. Even without paying for a hairdresser to do Little Sis's hair, Mummy still had to buy expensive products for mixed-race hair: a special shampoo and conditioner, hair grease and oils. Using a plastic baby doll several shades darker than Little Sis, Mummy taught herself how to plait hair in various styles to keep Little Sis's hair neat.

Little Sis would squirm and cry when Mummy was parting her hair into sections, greasing her scalp and plaiting her hair. Little Sis's hair was tamed at great pains. I felt sorry for Little Sis when Mummy got frustrated if she fidgeted too much and would hit her on the head with the comb in time with the words, 'Stay! Still!'

I asked Black and mixed-race schoolmates with plaits and braids, 'Does it hurt when your mum does that? Does she sometimes hit you if you don't stay still?'

'Yes, it hurts, but if it doesn't hurt, it's too loose and won't last,' they all said, or words to that effect.

The point of doing it tight was so that it lasted for a few weeks. My schoolmates told me they got more than a few taps on the head with the comb. They said they got 'licks' and 'beats' from their mums if they didn't stay still. Quizzing my peers reassured me Little Sis didn't have it so bad.

Mummy had only hit me once. It was non-uniform day, and my light blue Levi's denim jacket was taken from the school cloakroom. I'd hung my jacket up in the cloakroom and I didn't see how I could be held accountable for someone stealing it or taking it by mistake. Since it wasn't my fault, I was laissez-faire when I told Mummy the jacket had gone missing. Mummy slapped me across the face. She told me I had to look after my things and the jacket was expensive.

Time slowed.

I didn't understand how Mummy could've thought my jacket going missing was my fault. I had put it in the school cloakroom, the place where it was supposed to be put. My schoolmates and I had made and used a Ouija board in that cloakroom several times before because we thought it was haunted, but I didn't put the idea to Mummy that a ghost might be involved in the disappearance of my denim jacket. Was I supposed to guard it with my life, guard it from the dead, because Mummy had spent more money on it than she could afford to lose?

My cheek red with the sting of the slap, embarrassment, indignation and anger, I didn't turn the other cheek. I turned my eyes to Mummy. I weighed my words carefully before I spoke. I told Mummy I'd call Childline if she ever hit me again. A reminder more than a threat. Mummy was doing her best. She and I both knew violence was wrong.

Childline didn't get any calls from me about Mummy hitting Little Sis on the head with the comb. While it wasn't pleasant to witness, I didn't feel equipped to challenge it. I looked away, and as I stayed silent Little Sis learned to stay still. Soon enough, Mummy made light work of this once tricky task. No more hitting Little Sis on the head with the comb and no more tears.

When I went to the glass-fronted barbershop full of Black men without Mummy, I noticed that when there weren't women in the shop the conversation turned to vulgarities about sex and comments about the women who went past the shopfront window. They used words like 'batty man' to refer to gay and effeminate men. From their screwed-up faces I could see this phrase was hateful.

I took a keen interest in adult conversation and made conversation with adults from a young age. At Granny's I was told by aunts and uncles to keep out of 'Big People Talk'. But the use of the word 'batty man' in the barbershop made me wary of talking to any of the men there without having to be warned.

An awareness grew in me about what 'batty man' meant, what it might mean for me when I was a 'Big Man'. My hair stood on end every time I heard the words because, I'd realised, I was a 'batty man'. No tears. I wanted to cry but knew I couldn't because then they'd know for sure I was a 'batty man'.

I stayed silent. I felt afraid in that glass-fronted barbershop. The barbershop may have been a sanctuary to some, but it was a shark tank to me. I appeared to be absorbed in my Game Boy, so maybe these men didn't know I was listening to them.

These things were said by a minority of men in that barbershop, but the silence of the majority felt like a tacit agreement that women were to be gawped at, and gay and effeminate men were to be ridiculed. These sentiments were echoed in and echoes of the Jamaican dancehall music that blasted through the barbershop speakers.

My experience of Jamaicans was that we moved in family

groups. It wasn't uncommon for Jamaican boys and men to run errands with brothers or cousins.

'Follow me to the shop, cuz,' was a common refrain among my cousins.

Close family bonds? Strength in numbers? Could it be both? Could it be something else for other boys and men?

It never occurred to me that a man waiting for another man to get his hair cut could be his boyfriend. Even now at my 'Big Age' when I've accompanied my boyfriend, The Doctor, to get his hair cut at a Turkish barbershop, as The Doctor permitted the barber to singe off his ear hair but politely declined the offer of a shape-up for his thick caterpillar eyebrows, I've not looked at the men sat beside me waiting for another man in a barber's chair and thought they might be boyfriends as well. Instead, the smell of singed hair reminded me of The Irish Dancer and my attempt at having a girlfriend.

It never occurred to me as a child that adult men could've also been staying silent about their sexualities in order to stay safe at the barbershop. I arrived for my trim and fade, and I left silent and afraid. It felt like a slow death by a thousand cuts. My Game Boy was on mute but the pixelated words on the screen said, 'Game Over'.

Canerows

By the time I reached high school, I decided to grow my hair so Mummy could plait it. There would be pain, but it couldn't hurt more than the homophobia in the barber-shop. Mummy had mastered her hair-plaiting techniques on Little Sis, who perpetually looked school-photo-ready with brightly coloured bobbles at the end of her neat plaits.

I learned to withstand the pain when it was my turn for Mummy to plait my afro into canerows. This hairstyle was named after the neat rows of plaits which resembled the sugar cane fields my Jamaican ancestors may have been forced to work as enslaved people. I wore history on my head.

As she carefully parted and plaited my hair into neat sections, I enjoyed sitting on the floor between Mummy's legs and having her undivided attention, which I'd enjoyed for the eight years before Little Sis was born. When it was finished, the tight pull on my hair follicles was agony. Schoolmates told me the trick was to pat – but not scratch – my head to relieve the discomfort without messing up Mummy's handiwork. At night before bed, I wrapped my hair in a durag, which I also occasionally sported in the daytime underneath a baseball cap.

I had thought Yiayia cut Bapou's hair in their northwest London garden because Bapou couldn't afford to go to the barbershop, but now I wondered if it was an act of service, an act of love, from Yiayia to her husband. Plaiting our hair was one of Mummy's many acts of service for me and Little Sis. It was important to Mummy that Little Sis and I were well put together. She managed our Blackness through her care for our appearance and the first impressions we'd make in the world. Our golden-brown skin and plump pink lips moisturised and glistening with cocoa butter and Vaseline. Neat school uniform and neat hair.

My C of E high school didn't prohibit boys from having long hair, many white boys had long hair, but I wouldn't go to school without mine plaited into neat and careful rows. When I was fourteen, I refused to go to a house party because Mummy didn't get home in time to re-plait my hair. I'd taken it out of canerows and washed it in preparation for it to be redone. This was a birthday party for a girl from the lunchtime Bible study group, who were all white and conventionally attractive with straight hair, not a curl between them. Several of their fathers were vicars. The boys in this group played football or rugby for the school teams and the girls played hockey or netball. I was unsure if they were several couples or a group of platonic friends. My person in this group was my platonic friend and secret crush who played football most lunchtimes but would sometimes attend Bible study instead. I wasn't close with the others in the group, but they were perfectly pleasant when I went along at lunchtimes with or without Secret Crush.

I'd joined my C of E high school in the second year after an unhappy first year at Boy School, an all-boys' high school. An assistant headteacher had asked a snaggle-toothed spotty white boy with messy brown hair to look after me and show me around on my first day. This boy was gracious about doing this, he helped me get oriented and I couldn't help but develop a secret crush on him.

In his stature and personality, I could see the man he was going to become – kind, confident and strong. As I've said, Secret Crush played football most lunchtimes and I wasn't interested in joining in, so in my first few weeks before I'd made other friends, I'd watch him play. After school, Secret Crush and I meandered homewards together; we could've taken the bus, but we chose to walk and talk.

He was easy to talk to and one of his topics of interest was sport and fitness. He had weights and a bench press in his bedroom, and he invited me over to work out with him. I spotted Secret Crush as he lay on his bench press and lifted barbells, I felt the responsibility of taking the weight of the barbell should his arms falter. I examined his muscular white arms, his spotty red face, his bright white smile with its one snaggletooth. Secret Crush was attractive and confident, acne and all.

I told Secret Crush I was passionate about acting and that I'd performed on London's West End, at the Royal Albert Hall and Glyndebourne opera house. I told him about being on *Songs of Praise*. I'd also appeared on the children's TV show *Blue Peter* with the rest of the cast of the National Youth Music Theatre's production of *Bugsy Malone*, which earned me a coveted *Blue Peter* badge, a shield containing the *Blue Peter* sailing ship logo. Even with these impressive credits to my name, I lamented that I didn't get a leading role or solo.

'I wasn't good enough to be a star,' I said.

I told Secret Crush about the fourth of October 1996 when Michael Jackson came to see *Oliver!* at the London Palladium. I played a pickpocket in Fagin's gang. We had a post-show meet-and-greet on the stage with the safety curtain down. We lined up and, one by one, the King of Pop shook our hands.

I had Michael's albums on CD, cassette and vinyl, the

latter being hand-me-downs from my Cypriot uncle. I'd sung my heart out to 'Earth Song' with my primary school choir. I'd played 'Rock With You' on repeat at home. I had the *Michael Jackson's Moonwalker* video game for my Sega Mega Drive, along with *Aladdin*, *Mortal Kombat* and *Sonic the Hedgehog*. I'd even named my pet corn snake Ben after the Michael Jackson song about a rat. But I'd never thought about meeting Michael. It wasn't some far-fetched dream; it was an inconceivable thing. That day, he wore black aviator sunglasses, dark trousers, a black velvet jacket embellished with a jewelled sash on top of a white t-shirt or vest. It was over in a flash.

When Michael's photo was taken with his hands on the shoulders of the boys who played Artful Dodger and Oliver, I was stood a few feet behind them. I found myself in one Getty Images photo captured by photographer Dave Benett, but I'd been cropped out of all others. I was grinning but secretly gutted, a hollow empty feeling in my stomach that seemed to grow when I looked at that photo. While I knew Michael was a Black man with vitiligo stripping his skin of its melanin, I couldn't help but think his milky-white skin was closer in colour to the two white lead child actors than it was to mine.

It was my second year in *Oliver!* The first year I was in the workhouse and chorus. This year I was in Fagin's gang. Maybe it would've been third time lucky. Maybe if I'd done a third year, I could've been Artful Dodger or Oliver.

My inner child couldn't help but think if I had one of the leading roles, I would've got to stand side by side with the King of Pop. Although I didn't know the word for it back then, I believed in a meritocracy; I thought the main reason I didn't have a leading role in that musical was because I hadn't proved myself yet, I hadn't performed well enough. To my inner child it was nothing to do with racism or colourism, and it was nothing to do with luck. I simply wasn't good enough.

'I wasn't good enough to stand beside a star,' I said.

I told Secret Crush I still thought of myself as an actor and performer, but I didn't think of myself as a singer any more. When my voice broke my confidence shattered; my smooth soprano became a song of sorrow and self-pity.

I told Secret Crush why I'd turned down the role of Teen Angel in our school production of *Grease*: 'I auditioned for Danny – that was the only role I was interested in – it was leading man or nothing.'

Secret Crush told me if I wanted to be a 'leading man' I'd need to have a muscular body. He used Will Smith as an example. When I thought of Will Smith, I thought of *The Fresh Prince of Bel-Air*, when he was skinny as a beanpole. The first time I noticed Will Smith's body had changed was when he played Muhammed Ali in the film *Ali*. Actors got into the shape the role required of them. I'd get a personal trainer if I had to get fit for a role.

I wondered why Secret Crush chose Will Smith as an example rather than Leonardo DiCaprio or Johnny Depp, whom I believed were richer and more famous than Will Smith. I suspected Secret Crush had compared me to Will Smith because I'm Black.

Perhaps Secret Crush simply wanted to work out together to give us something to have in common besides us both having acne. Him: straight, white and sporty. Me: gay, Black and arty. He didn't look at me with desire. He saw potential. Our close friendship with little in common but precious time together prepared me for further close friendships with straight white men.

Mummy looked at me in a similar way to Secret Crush. She saw potential. When we went on summer holidays to Cyprus, she'd tell me how easy it would be for me to get six-pack abs by doing some sit-ups. Of all the things I wanted in life, six-pack abs weren't even in my top ten.

Secret Crush was the 'leading man' of my teens. With his bedroom workouts, Secret Crush was shaping the man he wanted to be. I wondered if he modelled himself after his footballing icons. I admired actors and music artists for their talent above and beyond their looks. I found some actors and music artists attractive, but this was a bonus. Justin Timberlake's shirtless 2003 *Rolling Stone* cover comes to mind. Hand on heart, I didn't think, I want a body like that. I thought, I want a boyfriend with a body like that.

My concerns were 'Will I ever get a boyfriend?' and 'Should I go to drama school or university when I finish high school?' My body didn't need to be worked on. It would get me to where I was going: a future in which I had a boyfriend and a career in the arts.

My high school was diverse but segregated when it came to groups of friends. A mixed-race butterfly boy, landing and leaving gently, I'd flit from group to group effortlessly. Sometimes I'd hang with the drama crowd, who were unconventional in various ways. At the forefront of this group were a white girl with braids, who was arguably the Drama Queen in her mannerisms and her penchant for gossip, and The Redhead, a cute skinny white boy with red curtains that fell in front of his eyes, causing him to flick his head to clear his vision.

If I wasn't at Bible study or in a drama rehearsal at lunchtime, I'd smoke cigarettes or weed with a group of girls who were Black, white, mixed-race and Asian. My Cypriot grandparents, Yiayia and Bapou, both smoked cigarettes, so smoking felt familiar. But seeing something and doing it are not the same. I'd cough and splutter and become the embarrassed centre of attention for a few moments. Otherwise, I was comfortably invisible in that cloud of smoke. I believed that smoking killed before they put words to that effect on the packet, but it was a risk I was willing to take in the pursuit of popularity and friendship.

Some girls in the lunchtime smoking circle had afro hair while others had straight hair. They'd all cycle through the same hairstyles regardless of ethnicity or hair texture; they'd have braids one week and pigtails the next. They'd talk about the boy they all fancied or the girl they didn't like that week because she was 'still a virgin' or 'such a slut'.

After school, if I was going to Yiayia and Bapou's, I'd travel with the Black boys who all chose to sit at the back of the top deck of the bus, afros, short back and sides with fades, a few other boys with canerows. They were a raucous bunch. Adults on the bus would tut and shake their heads at us. I sat still among the raised voices, friendly punches, backpacks flying across the aisles and litter thrown out of windows, but my brown skin and canerows were enough to make me part of the group.

Had it been someone from the drama crowd, one of the Black boys or weed-smoking girls hosting the house party, I might've gone with freshly washed fluffy curls. But a girl from lunchtime Bible study group was hosting the party the day Mummy was late for my home hair appointment.

I was looking forward to hanging out with Secret Crush. I was curious to see what the party of a girl from Bible study would be like. I suspected her vicar father would be supervising us all evening and there would be soft drinks and Christian rock music.

I dared to dream it could be a den of iniquity without adults or inhibitions. There would be alcohol, drugs and sex. There would be a game of spin the bottle with girls kissing girls and boys kissing me.

Which was it? I don't know, I didn't go.

I'd been to a wild party when I was eleven or twelve,

when I was attending Boy School. There were girls at the party. I don't know where they'd come from; they didn't seem to be anyone's girlfriends, least of all the girl thrust upon me.

Party Girl was blonde like Barbie and eager to kiss me. Party Girl tasted of sweet alcohol pop. We kissed for a long time without much conversation, and I didn't feel a connection.

I knew I was gay at eleven or twelve. Boy School was a stone's throw from Hampstead Heath. I'd heard that men met there for sex, and I thought I'd do that when I became a man. After school I'd pass Soho LGBTQ+ bars on my way to perform in *Oliver!* at the London Palladium, and I looked forward to visiting them when I became a man. I saw the gay milestones ahead of me, but I knew these activities were for men and not for an eleven- or twelve-year-old boy.

When Party Girl asked me why I spoke so posh, I said, 'I'm not posh, I just speak properly.'

When Party Girl asked if I wanted to have sex, I thought of the book Mummy had given me.

'I don't have condoms,' I said.

'We could use a plastic bag or something,' said Party Girl.

'No, I don't think so,' I said.

This was one of many troubling incidents in my year at Boy School. There was the older boy who made sexual advances towards me. The school camping trip with loud and exaggerated fake sex noises coming from tents that contained pairs of boys. The all-boys sleepover where other boys masturbated to straight porn that didn't turn me on. The 'don't drop the soap' jokes in the open-plan shower after P.E. And there was the group of boys who stood shoulder to shoulder to encircle me and another boy with long hair and yelled 'Fight! Fight! Fight!' Black Reebok Classics on every pair of feet. One thing I loved about Boy School was that you could wear these particular trainers instead of shoes.

Boy School was awash with blood and sweat but the tears had to be held back. There was a constant threat of physical and sexual violence. In my Reebok Classics I felt ready to run. But for some reason I didn't run.

I chose to fight. It was a one-on-one schoolyard fight, but he and I had no issue with each other, we didn't know each other. We were paired up to slog it out because we were effeminate boys. Who knows? Maybe if I'd made a different decision, he might've been my first boyfriend. I grabbed a fistful of his long straight hair and spun him in circles before I slapped him across the face. I turned my back on him and walked away. I was turning my back on a part of myself. I felt ashamed of my actions but also relieved that I'd won. Violence was wrong. I knew that. And yet when push came to shove, in a sink-or-swim situation, I was willing to push someone else down to save myself.

The absence of girls and the absence of religious guidance made me feel exposed and adrift at Boy School. For all these reasons and more, I'd left Boy School in favour of my C of E high school. But Reebok Classics hadn't been the only good thing about Boy School. I had a music place at Boy School, which meant clarinet and guitar lessons got me out of some regular classes. Boy School also let me leave early on Wednesdays to do matineé performances of *Oliver!* When I left, I missed wearing Reebok Classics to school, but I missed those music lessons most of all.

I most certainly didn't miss how the girl-hungry boys at Boy School told me Mummy was 'hot' and 'fit'. By comparison, at my co-ed C of E high school, a teacher mistook my young mum for a student. Mummy popped in to speak to one of my teachers, and on her way out, a P.E. teacher stalking the corridors hollered, 'Excuse me, young lady, what are you doing out of your lesson? Where should you be?'

'I'm a parent,' Mummy said meekly.

Mummy recounted this to me laughing and blushing. While being mistaken for a student may have embarrassed Mummy, I preferred this to the girl-deprived Boy School boys telling me how much they fancied her.

My C of E high school felt wholesome, like a home-coming. Still, the idea of going to a house party of straight-haired, strait-laced, presumably straight, white kids, when my afro was as fluffy as candy floss, filled me with anxiety. I didn't want to stand out. I was afraid that if I'd arrived looking like Sideshow Bob, the Christian rock music would cut off and everyone including Secret Crush would burst out laughing. No one had shown signs of cruelty in Bible study, but I didn't want to give them any chances. At fourteen, I tried to blend in with whatever group I hung out with. I was gay and building up the nerve to come out but until then I did my best to blend in.

Red

I tiptoed out of the closet at fifteen. In fairy-tale fashion, I thought a boyfriend would cure my depression. I had bouts of depression that had me bed-bound and missing days of high school, cocooned duvet days, a butterfly too weak to fly. I chose The Redhead from the drama crowd to be the object of my affections. I wrote him a letter to ask if he wanted to be my boyfriend. His response was as kind as it could be, but no less devastating to me. This heartbreak coupled with my depression was crushing.

How would I describe my depression to someone who hasn't felt it? In bed all day I'd drift in and out of sleep, restarting my sleep cycle again and again in a vain attempt to reboot myself, like when you've neglected your Tamagotchi virtual pet and it displays a digital grave on the pixelated screen and you have to press in the tiny reset button on the back of the plastic egg-shaped unit with a bent out of shape paperclip.

Deep down, I knew I only had one life and it was un-resettable. So, when I felt able, I'd do my best to make up for days lost in bed by working extra hard at school and being extra sociable, by performing at spoken word poetry events as well as talent competitions where I was up against rappers and singers and was sometimes declared the winner. During term time and school holidays, my life was awash with these activities.

I was under water in our baby blue bathtub which grew bigger and bigger around me until I was walking at the bottom of the ocean and the tub kept growing and the tap was running and running and I was too small to reach it even if I could swim to the surface and all I could think to do was pull the plug but I knew I couldn't or shouldn't do that so I'd have to learn to breathe underwater, and so I did, and so I do. That's how I'd describe my depression to you.

Thankfully, my actual and un-resettable pet, my corn snake Ben, felt real to me even when I didn't feel real to myself.

His quiet companionship, the way his red-brown body would coil around my golden-brown arm, the way he'd find his own way up to my shoulder and across my shoulder blades and down my other arm, and I'd pass him back to the first arm, catching a glimpse of his black and white checkerboard stomach. He'd do laps of my body, like he was charming me, circling my trunk like I was a tree, and he was chasing his own tail. When I changed his water daily, I checked his bedding for faeces and soiled patches, which I removed with disposable gloves. Once a month I replaced his bedding and cleaned everything in his tank.

I panicked and raised the alarm to Mummy the one time Ben escaped from his tank; after searching the entire house we found him in the kitchen coiled up behind the fridge. It was like I had lost and found a part of myself. If I were a witch, Ben would've been my witch's familiar. I kept volumes of the Encyclopaedia Britannica on top of the tank to prevent him lifting the lid again.

I could just about manage to take care of Ben. Although I provided him with food, water and shelter, I didn't provide him with the companionship of others like him. I believe Ben wanted to escape his tank to find others of his kind and explore and grow beyond the confines of captivity, like I'd escaped the shark tank of the barbershop, like I wanted to explore and grow beyond my own body.

Charmed by the serpent on my shoulder, I started to realise how little I needed to survive on days when I felt depressed, how little food, how little water, and how much school I could miss each term before it became an issue.

The Redhead confided in Drama Queen, which set off a chain of gossip. For the rest of the week, a procession of schoolmates asked me if I was gay. I said yes to everyone who asked, getting more confident each time because no one reacted badly. A one-word answer was enough to satisfy their curiosity about me. When they asked if The Redhead was gay too, I said, 'You'll have to ask him.'

I was the one out gay person in the whole school. Rather than a pariah, it made me cool. Secret Crush and the lunchtime Bible study group were even friendlier. One lunchtime they earnestly discussed close male friendships in the Bible. I found a sanctuary in this reading while I was still a virgin.

The weed-smoking girls started to ask me which boys I found attractive. The Black boys on the back of the bus didn't say anything negative about me. One of them told me I was 'brave' and he'd 'back me' if anyone said anything bad about me.

There was a whisper of homophobia in the air, but it barely reached me. By having friends in different groups in my year, I had allies everywhere. My peers watched what they said in front of me. If I was in the vicinity of someone who thoughtlessly said, 'That's so gay', about something they didn't like, they would quickly follow it up by saying, 'Sorry, Dean, I didn't mean it like that.' I'd pardon their slip of the tongue and move on.

The word 'gay' had many negative connotations, but I

gave the word another possibility for most of my peers. The gay boy in the school play. The gay boy at Bible study. The gay boy smoking weed. The Black gay boy at the back of the bus. I became more comfortable in my sexuality and in standing out.

My dream was that every LGBTQ+ – lesbian, gay, bisexual, transgender, queer, questioning or other – person at my high school would see me being Openly and Unapologetically Gay Every Single Day from then on. And hopefully seeing me might inspire them to be unapologetically themselves as well.

Coming out to Mummy was a kitchen sink drama. I was washing the dishes after dinner; focused on the task at hand, I was at one with the water when Mummy came into the kitchen and asked me why I was crying. I didn't know I was crying until then. I told Mummy about a boy at school who'd been whispering 'gay' under his breath in class and when he passed me in the corridor. I wasn't afraid of him. I knew he was trying to get under my skin. I both did and didn't care about this boy's opinion of me. I thought it rolled off me like water off a duck's back now that I was out. You know, sticks and stones and all that jazz.

It was such a cowardly form of bullying that I'd decided to ignore him, but the slow drip of one whispered word repeated over and over again was eroding the stony façade I presented to him. I could've reported him to the school-teachers or asked one of the Black boys from the back of the bus to have a word with him about the word he was calling me. Sobbing into the kitchen sink, I knew I'd let his homophobia go unchecked for too long. It hadn't rolled off me. Every time he whispered the word 'gay' it wounded me.

'Well, if you know it's not true, try not to let it get to you,' Mummy said.

'But it is true!' I wailed and threw myself to the checker-board lino floor, sobbing harder than before. A broken dam of months, if not years, of held-back tears.

Mummy sat beside me on the floor and stroked my back as I continued to cry.

'It's okay,' she said.

'I know,' I said.

Then she said, 'You have to be careful. You have to use condoms.'

She paused.

'Because of HIV,' she said.

'I know, Mummy,' I said. 'I know.'

Dread

'Do what makes you happy,' Mummy said.

I wanted to grow dreadlocks and had asked Mummy's opinion. As a sixteen-year-old, I didn't know what would make me happy.

So, I went with the flow and let my hair grow into locks, twisting it with beeswax to encourage it to knot.

Baptised and confirmed in the Church of England, I had no connection to the Rastafarian religion. Yes, I smoked weed and listened to Bob Marley, but I'd not seen any Rastafarians in my dad's Jamaican family. Still, I thought having dreadlocks would make me more Jamaican. I was grasping at straws to find my identity. And by straws, I mean spliffs. Bob Marley, weed and dreadlocks, that was all I could think of to show the world who I was.

The one man I knew with dreadlocks was Little Sis's dad, who was also of Jamaican heritage. He'd take Little Sis out every other weekend, while I'd go with Mummy to see her parents, my Cypriot grandparents, Yiayia and Bapou, or to see my dad's mum, Granny.

While my dad was a relative stranger with a short afro who made infrequent appearances in my life, Granny, my dad's mum, was stalwart in her love for me. Granny invited me to all the family gatherings and cut me a key to her house. My dad lived at Granny's and skulked around when I was there.

My dad was a spectre in my periphery. My peripheral vision and the outer limits of my life, even when we were in the same house. For reasons known only to my dad, he steered clear of me. He mostly stayed upstairs in his bedroom and if he came to the kitchen for a plate of food, he'd take it upstairs to his room again. I began to block my dad out of the corners of my eyes and focused on what was in front of me: Granny's abundant love.

My relationship with my dad was ambiguous at best. I didn't think he did anything a dad was supposed to do. Despite my emotional blinkers, it was painful to be ignored by him. I asked Black and mixed-race schoolmates about their dads; some talked of dads with tyrannical tempers, others didn't know their dads at all. I was surprised to find out several mixed-race schoolmates had a white dad and a Black mum, the opposite of me. One Black school-mate said he lived with his mum and dad, but his dad was like a ghost who sat in silence in an armchair all evening. Talking to my peers gave me comfort that my dad wasn't so unusual.

My dad's younger brother, Jamaican Uncle, was awash with cash. He bought me expensive gifts for my birthday and Christmas but, more than this, he showed up for me all year round. He has the appearance and affectations of TV chef Ainsley Harriott, shaved head and all. With a lilting RP English accent, he speaks with kindness and humour. He pokes fun at himself more than anyone else.

Jamaican Uncle drove a flash car like those I'd seen in music videos on MTV and The Box. He lived in a beautiful central London flat, but I didn't feel he kept it tidy enough to show its full glory. When I went to visit, I'd wash his dishes and plump the sofa cushions so I could see it looking show-home pristine, as if getting it ready for *MTV Cribs*.

I thought, One day I'll have a home like this.

On Christmas Day in my childhood and teens, I had lunch at noon with my Cypriot family, then at four in the afternoon I'd go to Granny's for a second meal. I didn't know if they waited for me or if they would have eaten at that time anyway. Despite the abundance of food, family and love, my dad's absence from the dining table was what I noticed most about Christmas. He'd collect his plate of food and take it back upstairs to his bedroom.

Granny stood at the head of the table in her good wig and said a prayer before we ate, in which she mentioned every family member at the table and those in Jamaica and elsewhere. 'Heavenly Father,' Granny began before she declared to God how thankful she was for his guiding hand in our lives, highlighting something we'd achieved or overcome that year. (Granny also prays this way on our birthdays. If we don't see her in person, she'll call us and pray over the phone.)

When I locked my hair, Granny prayed I'd cut it off. She prayed the police didn't mistake me for a drug dealer. She prayed I didn't get mixed up in any mix-up because of my dreadlocks.

I confess, I was thrilled that my locks filled Granny with dread, that she was worried about me for once. Granny's disapproval inspired my defiance and pride in my dread-locks. Granny didn't have favourites; she loved each of her children and grandchildren in the way we needed to be loved. But she did treat me differently to my other cousins, who were at hers more than me: she didn't raise her voice at me.

'It looks like you're not Granny's favourite any more,' said Cuz, the cousin I was closest to.

The rebel in me loved that.

At seventeen, I fancied myself a rebel and a revolutionary. I started writing and performing spoken word poetry. The first time I heard spoken word poetry was on a 1999 hip-hop album called *Things Fall Apart* by a band called The Roots. I was fourteen when this album was released and I knew songs from it like 'You Got Me' featuring Erykah Badu and Eve, but I didn't hear the album in its entirety until a few years later. There was a spoken word poem at the end of *Things Fall Apart*. I didn't know it was there until I got to the end of the album. There was a long silence and then a woman started speaking. She's not in the band, she was a guest on the album.

Her name was Ursula Rucker. She performed a poem called 'The Return to Innocence Lost'. It was the most harrowing thing I'd ever heard. It opens with a stark description of domestic violence and paints a painful picture of poverty. But her delivery was so powerful and beautiful, I rewound and listened to it again and again and again. When I found more of her work, I thought, *This isn't hip-hop. This is something else. This is poetry.*

There are only a few poems that have brought me to tears when I've read them on the page. But spoken word, when I discovered more of it on MySpace and YouTube and went to open mics around London, would have me sobbing into my sleeve. My favourite poets when I was younger were Gil Scott-Heron and Maya Angelou. Their work deals with dark subject matter and tough issues. It's frank, unashamed and empowering. I wanted to write like that, and that's what I began to do. I tried to write raw stuff that 'real people', people like me, could engage with. I tried to perform it in a way that I thought would engage people like me.

I had an acting background. I knew how to perform

well, how to put my whole body into my performance. But I had to learn to write well. That was my focus.

A poem I was most proud of back then was called 'Revolution'. With the standout line 'Silence is not golden; silence is the truth stolen,' it was speaking back to Gil Scott-Heron's 'The Revolution Will Not Be Televised', Linton Kwesi Johnson's 'Sonny's Lettah (Anti-Sus Poem)', Maya Angelou's 'Still I Rise', Tupac Shakur's 'The Rose That Grew From Concrete' and Ursula Rucker's 'The Return to Innocence Lost'.

The way I delivered 'Revolution' drew strength from the speeches of Martin Luther King Jr. and the trash-talk of Muhammad Ali. Bob Marley was an all-round influence on my writing, performance and appearance, as was the Black British writer, musician and self-proclaimed troublemaker Benjamin Zephaniah, who wrote about colonialism, politics, racism, veganism, and was Rastafarian with long thick dreadlocks. Benjamin was a fellow dyslexic who was encouraged to write when he was gifted a typewriter at a young age. Benjamin was also inspired by the music of Bob Marley.

My dreadlocks were my crowning glory. One summer I dipped them in lemon juice and sat out in the sun to bleach the tips blond. I wore a light blue denim shirt like I'd seen Bob Marley wearing. Visually, I fitted in with the Pan-African spoken word scene at small venues in Brixton, south London. Bars, restaurants and church basements would become spaces for Black consciousness. These venues would hold between thirty and one hundred people. Most were Black and many had dreadlocks, head wraps or afros. Many wore pendants or earrings in the shape of the African continent.

It was by listening to other Black poets with dreadlocks that I heard about the Lion of Judah and Haile Selassie I.

He was supposed to be the second coming of Christ. Since I'd stopped believing in the first, I had no time for the second. And yet I found myself joining in the call and response, along with the rest of the audience. If one of these poets called out 'Jah' I'd respond 'Rastafari'. In a similar way that at school I recited the Lord's Prayer, even though I didn't believe in God any more.

Some of my fellow poets sold homemade pamphlets, zines and CDs of their poetry, some sold homemade moisturisers and hair products. Some sold weed. Some sold it all. Eager to participate in this entrepreneurship I had t-shirts printed with the words 'SILENCE IS NOT GOLDEN' on and made this line into my slogan. An echo of the Silence=Death poster and project which mobilised to rally communities towards political action around the HIV/AIDS crisis in the eighties and nineties rather than remaining silent.

I was 'checking out me history' as John Agard says in his poem of the same name. I was checking out Black history. I was checking out LGBTQ+ history. I was incorporating it into my story. I would rewrite my story when necessary: I'd referred to myself as 'half-caste' until I heard the John Agard poem 'Half-Caste', which inspired me to rethink my vocabulary and use 'mixed-race' instead. Through writing and performing poems I began to claim Cypriot Greek and Jamaican patois as my own; there was more to me than RP English.

I was rethinking my personal brand: I was mixed-race and gay. I had dreadlocks on my head and my bold, gold-coloured 'SILENCE IS NOT GOLDEN' slogan emblazoned across my chest. My fellow poets called me 'Dread' and 'King' and I felt this was an acknowledgement of more than my locks. These special greetings made me feel special, like royalty or what I imagined royalty felt like.

When I performed spoken word poems about being gay, Black poets and audience members told me they respected me, told me I was 'brave'. This was a victory. It was everything I could've wanted from spoken word. I'd been afraid that the commonly held opinions about gay men were those I'd heard in the barbershop advocating the murder of 'batty men'. I didn't know anyone else who was Openly Gay in this Brixton spoken word scene. That didn't matter. Since I'd come out at school and at home, there was no stopping me from coming out at every opportunity. Silence was not golden; silence wasn't an option. I thought of how I'd not spoken up against the homophobia I'd heard at the barbershop and how I didn't want to stay silent about my sexuality any more.

Brixton had a reputation as a dangerous area, but I was comfortable there because I had a part-time job working as a cloakroom attendant for two music venues, Brixton Academy and Shepherd's Bush Empire, which I'd found out about from someone from the drama crowd at school. When I turned eighteen, in my last year of school, I graduated from working in the cloakroom to working behind the bar pulling pints and pouring spirits and mixers.

This job afforded me more than pocket money and free drinks. It meant I could tell Mummy I was going to work, even on a school night, and there would be no questions asked. My grades were good. I was taking Drama, English and Sociology at sixth form and had applied to read Philosophy & English at the University of Sussex. I was a man with an evolving personal brand and a loose plan: to do what makes me happy. Thanks to Mummy!

Between the two venues, I saw many amazing artists and bands, but the gig that stands out in my memory was Jamaican reggae and dub duo Sly & Robbie at Shepherd's Bush Empire in March 2003. The number of dreadlocked heads in the venue was astonishing. This 2,000-capacity venue was hot and sweaty, the air full of weed smoke and good vibes. I'd not seen this many Black people together anywhere besides Notting Hill Carnival, an annual celebration of Caribbean culture featuring sound systems and parade bands that has taken place in west London since the sixties.

Two people who stood out from the crowd of Black people queuing up for drinks at my bar: No Doubt lead singer Gwen Stefani and her husband Gavin Rossdale from the band Bush. I was too starstruck to speak to Gwen, I could barely look her in the eye.

'Your wife is so beautiful!' I said to Gavin.

'I know.' He smiled a brilliant white smile.

Gwen and Gavin looked like a life-sized Barbie and a bad boy Ken.

Sly & Robbie had featured on No Doubt's 2001 album, *Rock Steady*. I was a fan of this, their fifth studio album, and of songs on their third album, *Tragic Kingdom*. When *Tragic Kingdom* came out in 1995, I used to jump around Mummy's sala – 'living room' in Cypriot Greek – to the music videos for 'Don't Speak' and 'Just A Girl'. Imagining I was Gwen, my inner white woman with long blonde hair.

Rock Steady was a life-changing album; it celebrated Jamaican music in collaboration with many Jamaican producers and artists I'd heard on the barbershop speakers. No Doubt's mainstream success shifted something. I realised Jamaican culture was cool. Beyond the barbershop. Beyond Brixton. And beyond Bob Marley. It shouldn't have taken a white American to bring about this revelation, but it did. It wasn't until that autumn when I moved to Brighton for university that I started to take issue with the whitewashing of Jamaican culture.

King

'It's the poet,' my fellow students would say when they saw me around campus. I loved this! If I was to be known for anything, I wanted it to be for my poetry. I didn't tell my fellow students about the pet snake in my room because I didn't want to become known as 'the snake guy'.

Ben escaped from his tank once, but I didn't panic or raise the alarm. I found him coiled up behind the fridge in the communal kitchen just as I'd found him coiled up behind the fridge at Mummy's. Having left the Encyclopaedia Britannica at Mummy's, I put *The Complete Works of Shakespeare* on Ben's tank to prevent him lifting the lid again.

I'd moved to the University of Sussex in Brighton in the autumn of 2003. The African, Caribbean and Asian Society, ACAS, was a student union group that met once a week on a Thursday evening in a building called the Meeting House.

In a majority white university, city and country, ACAS was a sanctuary. They put on debates, film nights, potlucks and a monthly spoken word poetry event. I went to everything, but my appearances at the spoken word poetry events were my personal highlights. There was so much love and appreciation for my poetry that it became my whole identity. Poetry was my priority.

I also joined the drama society and acted in two productions with them – *Beautiful Thing* by Jonathan Harvey, the play from which the film was made, and *Shopping and Fucking* by Mark Ravenhill – but no one said 'It's the actor' when they saw me around campus. I could act, for sure. But I wasn't an actor. I was 'the poet'. I arrived at university a poet, and a poet is what I remained.

Some things did change about me.

At ACAS I heard the term 'political blackness' for the first time, an umbrella term that arose in the UK in the seventies, which meant you could refer to anyone likely to face discrimination on the basis of skin colour as 'black' with a small 'b'. On these terms, 'black' could mean anyone who wasn't white. 'Political blackness' had gone out of fashion by 2003 when I started university, but it was alive and well in ACAS. I saw myself in this older but new-to-me concept of blackness.

'What's up, my nigga?'

He was the first and only person to call me the n-word to my face. He was an Asian member of ACAS. I heard an 'a' and not an 'er' ending. I knew he believed this to be a term of endearment. But it didn't feel endearing. It felt humiliating coming from him.

'Don't ever call me that again,' my words punched through gritted teeth. I turned my back on him and walked away. We rarely spoke after that day.

As I became closer friends with the Black and mixed-race women of ACAS, I began rethinking my personal brand again. I started to refer to myself as 'Black' in addition to 'mixed-race' in conversations with these women. They fed me African and Caribbean food and twisted my dreadlocks with beeswax to keep my roots neat after my weekly hair wash. Acts of friendship. Acts of service. I sat between their legs, the way I used to sit between Mummy's legs when she'd plait my afro back into neat canerows. We adorned a select few of my dreadlocks with silver-coloured hair beads, enough to be noticed but not so many that they'd knock against one another when I bounced around campus or danced in a club. My dreadlocks accentuated the natural spring of my step and sway of my hips.

Taking the presidency of ACAS was a minor coup. I gathered the select few women I was closest to, and we formed an executive committee to present a united vision for ACAS and run on a joint ticket rather than as individual candidates. I trusted these women to share my vison because of how well they'd taken care of me since we'd arrived at university. We allocated the roles of vice president, treasurer, etc, until we had a full executive committee. We ran for election unopposed.

I felt emboldened. Black enough. Unapologetically Gay. I became the Black students' rep on the students' union council. Even though I manoeuvred to make this happen, it felt natural, it felt destined to be; I felt leadership suited me.

I felt free. Some friends and I made a documentary in which we asked ACAS members and other students what freedom meant to them. We screened it on campus on Freedom Day 2004, commemorating twenty years since the first post-apartheid elections held in South Africa on 27 April 1994.

I felt audacious. I didn't interrogate my light-skinned/mixed-race privilege. I amplified my intersectionality: I was Black *and* gay! I had these grand ideas of myself as the Black gay councilman and the Black gay president.

My dreadlocks carried a natty knotty history and an expectation that the man who wore them would conduct himself as a 'King'. So, when white people touched my dreadlocks without permission it felt treasonous. I was a 'King', and they were snatching at my crown. I felt a knot in my stomach. I didn't mind when my arse cheeks were cupped or my dick was grabbed when I danced with men in clubs, I enjoyed and encouraged that contact, but if their hands strayed into my hair, I felt violated.

These violations clung to my hair like the stale stench of cigarette smoke that had coiled its way into my dreadlocks. Before the indoor smoking ban, clothes and hair smelled of cigarette smoke after nights out at bars and clubs. Clothes could be changed, but I couldn't wash my dreadlocks every day, so I'd use a lavender-scented spray to spruce them up in the meantime between my weekly hair wash. When I sprayed that lavender scent in my hair, I imagined a garland of real lavender on my head, a green and purple crown atop my brown and blond dreadlocks with their silver-coloured hair beads.

No one besides Granny had ever said anything disparaging about my dreadlocks, but in Brighton I became aware they weren't working in my favour. I saw so many white people with dreadlocks around campus and in the city. I saw so many white people with dreadlocks smoking weed on Brighton beach and in the reggae clubs where there were barely any Black people.

I wasn't aware of the term 'cultural appropriation', but I felt uncomfortable with white people having dreadlocks. Granny's fears were made manifest. I was mistaken for a drug dealer in Brighton. White people at house parties, in the student union bar, in clubs and on Brighton beach would ask me if I was selling weed. I'd go to the pebble beach to sit and meditate with the waves, but I couldn't relax. I had to have my wits about me because I stood out in a way I didn't want to.

In ACAS, I didn't need dreadlocks to signal my Jamaican roots. I didn't need to consume white versions of Jamaican culture to be proud of my heritage.

The signals I thought I was sending and the signals that people were receiving were getting mixed up. My crown began to weigh me down. My dreadlocks no longer served me. Their history and expectations were too great for me to carry. I cut them off in my bedroom with kitchen scissors.

I let my hair grow into an afro. This time I didn't wear it plaited back in canerows. I wore my hair freely for the first time. Even though I'd had long hair before, I'd kept it plaited because I'd been embarrassed of its mixed texture.

My afro didn't fall in loose golden-brown curls like that one mixed-race boy of my childhood. It did different things on different days and sometimes it had four different textures at once: fluffy candy floss, soft lamb's wool, tight silky curls and some strands straight. Some days I thought it looked beautiful and others I thought I looked like a troll doll. My afro stood up. My afro stood out. Nonetheless, I wore my mixed-textured afro proudly, and I confidently said no when white people asked if they could touch my afro. My hair and confidence grew, as did my repertoire of spoken word poems – and my poetry got me invited to places I'd never imagined it would take me.

Growing

In sociology at high school, I'd learned about 'cultural capital', which can be embodied, institutionalised and objectified. Accent and etiquette are examples of embodied cultural capital. Institutionalised cultural capital could be a university degree. Objectified cultural capital can be found in objects of culture such as owning a piece of art. Cultural capital can also be found through experiences such as going to the theatre, to museums and galleries, and going on holidays. I'd had many such experiences.

I had an abundance of cultural capital. I leveraged this during the two decades of financial precarity I faced after my undergraduate degree. I networked with arts workers and gatekeepers at theatre press nights, exhibition openings, film screenings, and at private members' clubs as someone's plus one or on the guest list in my own right.

I sold talent and time with the goal of being able to afford to move out of Mummy's, but never at the expense of my dream of being a writer. My biggest privilege was living in London, the capital city of England and the UK, where opportunities in the arts were abundant for those willing to apprentice or intern or indeed work for free for 'exposure', which I did for many years.

I kept writing poems and my hair and confidence kept growing. I wore my afro to read a poem at the Houses of

Parliament to commemorate the life and death of Nelson Mandela. I wore my afro to meet Queen Elizabeth II at Buckingham Palace. I wore my afro to meet Prime Minister Gordon Brown at 10 Downing Street and Mayor of London Boris Johnson at City Hall. In addition to my afro, I was rocking a long, full beard like a Greek Orthodox priest when I went to meet David Cameron at 10 Downing Street.

Granny told me I favoured my father, meaning I looked like my dad. This was a painful comparison for me. When my face was clean-shaven, I could see him, which was why I'd decided to grow a beard. I was impressed with my beard. It wasn't neat. It wasn't full at my cheeks, but it grew long and bushy.

I remembered first shaving in my teens, an attempt to make the whiskers above my top lip grow back into a full moustache. I used an orange and white Bic razor Mummy kept on the side of the baby blue bathtub. Red polka-dotted the baby blue sink. I looked in the mirror at my unfortunate blood moustache. Even with my face bleeding, I was hopeful that one day I'd have a full beard, and that when I looked in the mirror, I wouldn't see my dad looking back.

At the gate to Downing Street, a colleague said I might not get past the security checkpoint and armed police because I looked like a terrorist. I wanted to slap that colleague across the face with my pre-Brexit burgundy passport. Instead, I pulled my colleague up on his comment, but he insisted it was banter, a joke. But this throwaway comment got me thinking. My afro may have become acceptable in institutional settings, but my beard was pushing the gilded envelope.

On a white man of my age, then or now, a long, full beard will read to many as a hipster style. On a Black or brown man, a similar long, full beard may read to some as a threat. I'm not Muslim, but what that colleague said was an Islamophobic trope about Black and brown men with long, full beards.

My hair was more than a personal choice. My hair was political. Whether or not I was aware, my hair was inevitably and constantly sending out signals. Respectable with short back and sides. Neat with canerows. Rasta with dreadlocks. Proud with an afro. 'Terrorist' with a beard.

The assumptions people made based on my hair weren't all accurate, but to deny their impact on my life would be foolish. For Black and brown people, our hair is wrapped up in many isms and phobias. There's no doubt about that.

Now I keep my hair cropped and my beard short and neat, I feel less conspicuous, less political in appearance. One might say I look more distinguished. It feels like a gift of ageing that hairstyles matter less to me. The rebellions of my teens and twenties were necessary for me at the time. Being the subject of banter and disapproval has not been limited to my choice of hairstyle; growing up Black and queer in a predominantly straight white country I've had to learn to stand up tall with or without an afro.

Hairy Crack

'Oh my, you have a hairy crack!'

I was face down on his bed, and this was the first thing he said upon seeing my arse crack. I was in my early twenties when I met this curly-haired comedian.

'I beg your pardon?'

I couldn't believe my ears. My head was still ringing. I thought I had concussion. I'd been so eager to have sex with The Comedian that I'd thwacked my head on the gate to his building complex. I pulled it towards me with all my might when he'd released it. The slapstick of this had been embarrassing but felt an appropriate prelude to sex with The Comedian. Never mind my bruised ego and throbbing head, what had The Comedian just said about my crack?

'Your crack. It's very hairy,' he repeated.

This comment would come back to me over the years as more and more sexual partners requested that I shave my arse crack, chest and pubes.

And the Category Is . . . Body Hair!

My willingness to remove my body hair would depend on how much I desired the man doing the asking and how much I needed them to desire me. Without body hair, I fit the gay stereotype of a 'twink': young, slim with boyish looks. With body hair, I reluctantly found myself categorised as an 'otter': lean build with a layer of face and body hair which is sometimes referred to as 'scruff'. I first encountered these words when looking online for gay porn in my teens and again when using gay dating websites and on the apps when they came along. I self-selected the category 'otter' to avoid surprise or comments about my body hair.

Other categories that pay attention to body hair include 'wolf': lean or muscular and semi-hairy; 'bear': stocky, with a rotund belly and an abundance of body hair; 'cub': also stocky with body hair but younger than a bear. 'Bear' and 'cub' types operate in relation to each other, whereby the younger is the 'cub' of the older 'bear'.

There are also categories such as 'clean-cut', 'discreet', 'geek' and 'jock' that use other traits to stereotype men. Not all are animal references, but all are reductive and lack meaningful nuance. If you know the category or type you fit into, you can play up to it to find people who'd want to have sex with you. If not an unlimited choice, there was certainly an abundance of cock and arse available to me. Not only those who lived in and around London but also tourists and those on work trips.

'As long as I can fit into one of these categories, someone somewhere will be into me,' I often told myself, on days when I didn't feel attractive.

The categories of 'cub' and 'bear' were beacons of hope in my early thirties when I gained weight. Those categories meant I'd still have a place in gay hook-up culture even if I was categorised and fetishised because of my body hair and size. At thirty-six, I'm still an otter but may be on my way to becoming a bear.

There are other ways to describe my body beyond these categories. 'Thick' and 'dad bod' are two that spring to mind, but like Goldilocks I'm looking for something that's 'just right'. 'Otter', 'cub' and 'bear' do feel right for a body like mine, a body with an abundance of hair.

My boyfriend, The Doctor, is also an otter. Perhaps a wolf because of his lean, muscular physique.

'Do you prefer my body hairy or shaved?' he asked when we first became boyfriends.

It was a loaded question. I didn't want to have an opinion. I prefer him hairy, but I told him he should do what makes him happy. An echo of Mummy's advice to me about my dreadlocks and life in general. When The Doctor shaves his body hair, he's no less attractive. If anything, it's a novelty. It's like I'm in bed with a different man for few days.

'What's your type?' was another question The Doctor asked early on. People ask this to see how they measure up against the people you're typically attracted to.

The Doctor is white-passing with English and Mediterranean heritage. Roman Catholic upbringing. Private school education. He has olive skin, a large nose and large ears, and hazel eyes under thick caterpillar eyebrows. He looks awkward when he tries to smile for a photo, but he has a lovely smile if it occurs naturally. He's seven years younger than me and has a lean muscular body, as I've said. He has thick, dark, straight hair. Short back and sides, a wayward mess up top, and natural wisps of blond at his crown like a streak of golden light forever descending upon him. Despite his not using hair gel or any other setting agent, his hair sits in natural clumps like the fronds of a palm tree, or the feathers of a bird caught midway through a courtship display.

'Redheads have been my type, historically,' I told The Doctor. I said 'historically' as if I was talking about centuries ago rather than ten years ago.

When I asked what his type was, The Doctor said he didn't have one. It hadn't occurred to me that it was an option to lie and pretend I didn't have a type. I knew I'd made a mistake by telling The Doctor what my type was.

It began with The Redhead at school. Even though he said no when I asked him out, I subsequently had three redhead boyfriends.

By the time I was on my third redheaded boyfriend, close friends noticed the pattern and it became a running joke that I exclusively fancied redheads. I didn't. I fancied Black men, mixed-race men, blond and brunette white men too. I felt embarrassed that anyone might think I only fancied redheads because it made my skin crawl when white people told me they only fancied Black and mixed-race people.

I didn't know if I could say 'ginger'. One of my redhead boyfriends said, 'Ginger is a slur.' He said, 'Having red hair is like being Black because people judge you before they know you.' He said, 'Ginger is an anagram of the n-word.' Now I roll my eyes but at the time I let it slide.

All three of my redheaded boyfriends told me they'd been bullied in school about their red hair and freckles. They found it ironic that as adults these were things people found attractive about them. Some redheaded people feel they are fetishised for the colour of their hair.

'What do you think of him?' The Doctor would ask when we passed a redheaded man in the street, or saw one in a bar, restaurant, film or TV show.

I've experienced from all sides how skin colour, hair colour and hairstyles can be fetishised. I've felt fetishised in the gay community, especially when people touched or made comments about my dreadlocks or afro hair when chatting me up.

I did have a fetish for redheaded men. I also had a fetish for white men who sang R&B. Black music from a white body. Two of my redheaded boyfriends were R&B singers. Make of that what you will.

Queens

In my twenties I hung out with actors, dancers, DJs, drag queens, models, musicians, music producers and fellow poets all over London. Most weekends and some weeknights too, I was on the guest list for clubs in Brixton, Shoreditch and Soho. These spaces were sanctuaries. They were LGBTQ+ friendly, if not LGBTQ+ led.

My good friend Mr DJ was friends with music producer, club promoter and drag queen Jodie Harsh. Mr DJ would get me on the guest list for Jodie's club night Circus, which was sentinelled by glamazonian drag queens, hostesses and party-starters. Besides Jodie, whose name and face were on all the publicity, I don't remember the names of the other queens.

They were dotted around the club, some with their own seating booths sectioned off behind red velvet rope. They had huge hair, stunning makeup and danced in high heels, much to my astonishment. Some looked seven foot tall in their heels and wigs. They towered over me. I felt insecure in their company. Witnessing their self-expression, I felt inspired and afraid about what it might mean for me to do drag. I didn't dare approach them. I was afraid their courage would rub off on me and put me in danger. I was afraid of my own effeminate nature. The drag hostesses didn't invite me to their booths. I was a VIP in the most exclusive section of the club: the DJ booth.

Despite zero degrees of separation between Jodie and me, all I managed to say to her was 'hello' and 'thanks for having me'. Her hair stayed stock-still as she bopped her head in time with the tunes she was spinning. She wore a signature blonde wig with dark roots that signified 'bleached blonde'. Her hair rose a foot in the air before sweeping down in a cascade of waves over her shoulder. Her hair was like the crest and the trough of a wave suspended. Her eyes framed with thick black lashes and eyeliner, the colour on her eyelids would match an element of her outfit: electric blue, silver or gold. Jodie was and is a superstar, and to be in her presence for one night a month filled me with a sense of acceptance and privilege I didn't feel in other clubs where I was one of many unknown bodies on a meat market dancefloor.

I stayed by Mr DJ's side. He put me on the guest list and handed me drinks tokens. Mr DJ was tall, white, slim, masculine presenting. He had dark hair and piercing blue eyes, he had his own initials tattooed in cursive on his neck. He wore black t-shirts, a black leather jacket and Vivienne Westwood jewellery. He was the epitome of style.

Throughout my teens and into my twenties, Mummy bought me the clothes I requested for my birthday and Christmas, whether that was a Burberry shirt or Ed Hardy jeans, but I always felt like I missed the trend when my friends moved onto something new. What Mr DJ wore was timeless and classic. We didn't have a sexual relationship, but I certainly found him attractive. He had arrestingly good looks and a heart of gold. I didn't reveal my attraction to him for several reasons. One, I was certain it wasn't reciprocated. Two, he was such a good friend, and I didn't want to make things awkward. Three, he was a cigarette smoker, which I could accept in friends and family but not in someone I'd be locking lips with.

My favourite Circus residency was at Paramount on the thirty-first and thirty-second floors of Centre Point on Tottenham Court Road. If you stuck it out for the whole night, you were rewarded with panoramic views of the sun rising over central London. I'm grateful I could take guest lists and free drinks for granted. I wasn't earning much money from poetry but all I needed was enough on my Oyster card. London was my oyster. These nights were the pearls.

At a different club with Mr DJ, I was introduced to Jay in the smoking area. Jay seemed painfully shy. He could barely look me in the eye. When he said 'Hello', he looked down.

'So, who's Jay?' I asked when Mr DJ and I were back on the dancefloor. I thought maybe he was one of Mr DJ's past or future conquests.

'What are you talking about?' Mr DJ laughed. 'That's Jodie. You've met her a million times.'

While I had met Jodie many times, I'd not met Jay.

'But he's so shy,' I said.

'That's why he invented Jodie,' said Mr DJ.

Fast-forward a decade.

'A man in a dress.'

This was how Michael Twaits referred to himself. His ten-week course demystified drag and opened my eyes to its unlimited possibilities. Curious about the transformative power of drag, in January 2017 I signed up for The Art of Drag, run by Michael at the Royal Vauxhall Tavern, a Grade II-listed LGBTQ+ entertainment venue. I knew the venue because I performed my poetry at their Tuesday cabaret, Bar Wotever, and Saturday club night, Duckie.

Bar Wotever was the first place I was asked what my pronouns were.

'I don't know what that means,' I confessed to the compere.

'How would you like me to introduce you to the stage: he/him, she/her, they/them, any other pronouns or no pronouns and just your name?'

'Are they allowed to ask you that?' said a voice in my head that sounded like Mummy.

'He/him?' I said as if this was still in question.

Drag traditionally privileges men in dresses, whether comical like Lily Savage and Dame Edna or glamorous like RuPaul and Jodie Harsh. Although there are many drag kings, drag queens, trans, non-binary and genderqueer drag performers, the majority of drag performers you saw on TV shows like *Drag Race* or at drag nights across the UK were men in dresses. I signed up for Michael's course thinking I wanted to be taught how to be one of the glamorous ones, the glamazons, but I soon realised drag was going to take me in a different direction.

It was March 2017, and I had less than a month left to finalise the look for my drag debut. I had chosen the name for my drag persona, The Black Flamingo, but I was yet to decide what that would look like. The character was gifted to me by a news report of a real black flamingo sighting in Cyprus when I was visiting my family there in 2015.

I had elements of my act together: a poem from the perspective of The Black Flamingo who wants to be pink; lip syncs to 'Flamingo' by Kero Kero Bonito, an upbeat song about eating pink shrimp to turn your skin pink; and the Beyoncé cover of Amy Winehouse's 'Back To Black'. I wanted to take the audience on a journey from one to the other. I borrowed black feathers and a black tutu from Michael's own drag wardrobe. I borrowed a pink fur coat from another friend. The pink fur coat was almost floor-length, so I could wear anything or nothing underneath.

In the privacy of my bedroom, I modelled the pink fur coat and my newly purchased four-inch-high black heels. The fur coat was lined with a silky material and the feel of it on my naked hairy body as I ran my hands across the fur of the coat was a sensory, bodily revelation. From this private, intimate moment, I tried to develop something I'd be happy to do in public, in front of an audience of strangers, friends and family.

Drag is about layers and textures, of meaning as well as of makeup and clothing. I wasn't prepared to invite the audience to touch my body, but I wanted to stimulate the major senses: sight, smell, sound, taste and touch. I'd stimulate sight with colour. I came up with the idea of going from a pink costume to a black one, through a striptease in keeping with Beyoncé's sultry singing on 'Back To Black'. That was sound sorted. For taste, I'd hand out pink sweets to the audience. If a colour could have a smell, the strawberry-flavoured jelly foam shrimps I picked were pungently pink. This idea came from my other lip sync song, 'Flamingo' by Kero Kero Bonito. Handing out these sweets from a raised stage would be a queer communion. Touch without touch. Not my body but embodying me. Christ-like energy. I'd choose an audience member to pour a glass of rosé wine for, and then I'd drain the rest of the wine from the bottle.

I had no idea what to do regarding my hair. I'd said 'goodbye' to my afro. I'd accepted it was thinning at the crown and receding at the front. I'd rubbed argan oil into my scalp for a year to promote hair growth. I'd tried to style my afro swept across to one side to cover my balding crown.

When the wind blew, it would reveal the bald patch, and

the cold air touching my scalp sent a shiver down my spine from head to toe. Deep down. Bone deep. To my core. I felt insecure around tall people, anxious of how I looked from above. I felt the 'spotlight effect'; I believed everyone cared as much as I did about my balding. I knew in my marrow that if I was going to step into the spotlight as The Black Flamingo then my thinning hair had to go.

I drew a blank when it came to hairspiration for my drag persona or alter ego. The final image I had in mind was standing triumphantly in a spotlight with my hands on my hips and black feathers on my shoulders, a smile on my face with hair cropped and my beard short and neat.

Once I'd decided the journey of my drag performance would end with my own cropped hair, it followed that I had to begin by wearing a pink wig. I'd wear the pink wig and fur coat, then reveal The Black Flamingo, proudly standing out from the crowd, even when that meant standing alone.

I went to a hair shop in Brixton Market to find a pink wig for under twenty pounds. The shop had wall-to-wall mannequin heads in wigs and packs of human and synthetic hair hanging on hooks like an abattoir, a slaughterhouse of wigs and weaves ready to slay another day.

I chose a bob-style pink wig because it reminded me of the Black rapper Lil' Kim and the dancers I'd seen in the 1997 Jamaican film *Dancehall Queen* and countless dancehall music videos. Brightly coloured hair may have been a way for these women to stand out and be noticed. My pink wig represented blending in. I'd remove it and toss it on the floor during my performance when I rejected pink and embraced black.

I spent a lot on makeup. The person who gave me the makeup tutorial in the department store convinced me I needed eyelid primer, face primer, concealer, foundation, powder, eyeliner, lipliner, lip gloss, eyeshadow palettes and a brush set to apply it all. Luckily, I had set aside some money from the discount Michael Twaits had given me on the price of The Art of Drag course.

I saw several performances by sensational drag performer, singer and all-round queer icon, Le Gateau Chocolat, who says of himself, 'Before I'm gay, black and fat, I'm human. My work is about that.' His solo show *Black* tells his story of coming to the UK from Nigeria and charts his hopes, fears and battle with depression in his own words and a reworking of my favourite song, 'I Wanna Dance with Somebody (Who Loves Me)'.

Le Gateau's sixty-minute masterpiece covering three decades of his life gave me permission to put my life-long battle for self-acceptance into my ten-minute debut drag performance. That he is Black, fat and keeps his beard and chest hair to do drag, gave me permission to put on that pink wig and a full face of makeup, keeping my beard and body hair untouched. It felt liberating not to shave the hair on my face or body to fit a conventional drag aesthetic.

As my drag persona, The Black Flamingo, I walk on stage in glittering pink Converse boots. I wear a pink wig and a pink fur coat. Underneath I have on a black leotard, black tutu and sheer tights through which my hairy legs can be seen. My legs look incredible in an unconventional way. I wear a figure-hugging costume but without a corset or pads to give myself an hourglass shape. I proudly parade my natural curves.

Midway through my drag performance, I throw off my pink coat to reveal my black costume, whip off my pink wig and exchange my glittering pink Converse for black high-heeled shoes. I go from one type of fabulous to another, by way of self-acceptance. Both costumes look good. The transition from one to the other tells my story of wanting to blend in with the pink flamingos but instead becoming proud to stand out as a black flamingo.

My final silhouette is constructed on stage as if to say to the audience: 'I transformed myself right before your eyes. I didn't hide any part of the process. And this is me now, standing tall, here to be celebrated. A Black, queer, flamboyant, bearded beauty, basking in the spotlight and bold enough to ask for your applause because to applaud me is to applaud a world with so many more possibilities.'

But wait.

Was I doing drag to become an unbelievable beauty, a stereotypical hyper-feminine parody? Was I doing it for my inner child? My mixed-race butterfly boy? Did I want to become the Barbie doll he hid from the other boys? Did I want to release my inner white woman? My inner Black female rapper? My inner Jamaican dancehall queen? Was that it? Was that my goal?

Not at all. My goal was to look beyond MTV and think outside The Box. I didn't want to be a life-sized Barbie doll. I wanted to be unconventional. I wanted to wear the crown of a drag queen on my own terms: a liberated Black, queer, hairy body in the spotlight. Hands on hips, head held high, and striking red lipstick framing a bright white smile.

Make no mistake. The Black Flamingo is a character, a persona or alter ego I invented, a mask I wear on stage to say and do the things I'm too afraid or ashamed to say and do as Dean. Like Jodie Harsh is for Jay, The Black Flamingo is an elevated version of me, a projection of who I'd like to be, perhaps. The Black Flamingo is not the person I am inside.

The Black Flamingo is a character, a persona or alter ego I hide behind. Drag was a cocoon, a second skin that I could shed with coconut oil and makeup wipes. I let go of impermanent parts of myself when I removed my makeup and false eyelashes after each performance as The Black Flamingo; as I saw my bare face, the bags under my eyes the concealer had concealed, the grey in my beard that an unconventional application of black mascara had hidden, and my cropped crown with its receding hairline that I knew I'd have to learn to accept but hadn't yet. I didn't allow myself to wear makeup or hide my grey hairs outside doing drag. I was afraid I wouldn't learn to love my ageing face if I carried on covering it up with makeup. I was afraid I wouldn't learn to love my greying and balding self if I didn't throw away my bottle of argan oil and accept my crown.

SIGHT

Laser Eye Surgery

Mummy paid for one eye as a birthday gift. I paid for the other as a gift to myself. I had laser eye surgery in November 2016, a week after my thirty-second birthday. Before surgery I was short-sighted, −9 and −8.5.

I'd wanted laser eye surgery from when I first heard about it in the nineties, but I had to wait for three things: to become an adult, to be able to afford it and to feel confident that it was safe. By the time I had my surgery in 2016 it was considered one of the safest elective surgical procedures available and there was only a one in five million chance of being blinded by it.

Despite this statistic, I was afraid. I'd researched. I'd waited and waited some more. I'd asked all my questions at my consultation with the surgeon and was satisfied with his answers. The surgeon told me this procedure wouldn't fix my vision for ever and I may need glasses again by the time I reached forty. Eight years into the future was unfathomably far. What worried me was that tiny possibility – one in five million – of being blinded by the surgery. As the back of my chair was lowered to lie me horizontally, I gripped the armrests.

As the laser beam shot into my first eye, I was terrified I'd be blinded. I believed I was unlucky enough to be that one in five million. My eyeball melting, the laser beam burning clean through my skull.

'That's your first eye done. Are you ready for the second?' said the surgeon.

I'd opted to get both eyes done in the same session rather than doing one eye and letting it heal and coming back to do the other. When the laser was shut off after the second eye was done, I was handed dark glasses to keep on for two weeks as my eyes would be extra sensitive to light while they healed. These glasses were more like darkened swimming goggles because they sat flush to my face and didn't let light enter my eye from any direction.

Two weeks of wearing these darkened goggles like I'd sunk to the bottom of the ocean. I was a shell of myself, stuck in my bedroom, navy blue curtains closed, listening to podcasts and audiobooks. I went back to have my eyes checked and tested. It was a successful surgery without complications.

I came out of my shell. I was liberated from contact lenses and glasses. I could club all night and go home with whomever I liked without worrying about carrying my contact lens case and solution. I could wake up and see with no need to feel my way around for my glasses. I could go to hot yoga in a heated studio and sweat to my heart's content without glasses steaming up or contacts irritating me. I could finally see clearly.

Queer Eye

I asked my schoolteacher if I could move closer to her. I couldn't see the board from my designated seat at the back of the class. My short-sightedness was recognised in primary school, and after my first eye test I received a pair of free prescription glasses in plastic frames.

I liked my glasses because I could see the board and participate in class. That's what mattered most in primary school. I didn't become self-conscious of my appearance until high school when I developed acne. Going through puberty and becoming increasingly aware of my sexuality, I was horrified looking in the mirror at a face full of spots through plastic frames and lenses that magnified the size of my eyes.

I asked Mummy to take me to the GP for acne treatment and I asked if I could swap my glasses for contacts. Mummy obliged on both counts. The acne medication, a daily pill and an ointment to apply at night was free on the NHS, but the contacts came at a cost.

I can't remember if it was Mummy who paid for my contacts or whether I paid for them from money I had saved up from my musical theatre jobs in London's West End, at the Royal Albert Hall and Glyndebourne opera house. What matters is there was a decision to start spending more money on my appearance. I still wore glasses much of the time because I didn't enjoy sticking my finger in my eyes to put my contacts in; when I did have them in, I found them irritating. This discomfort was a hidden cost.

Before this point, I'd unquestioningly worn clothes Mummy bought, and my freedom of self-expression regarding my appearance consisted in how I asked the barber to cut my hair. Before puberty I didn't dress hoping other boys would find me attractive, didn't look in the mirror and grimace; before puberty, my skin was smooth and golden brown. I smiled at myself in the mirror. My self-image unblemished. I saw myself simply. I simply saw myself.

During puberty, I constantly thought about what other boys saw when they looked at me. I was comparing myself to them; their height, weight, muscles, haircut, body hair, facial hair, clothes, even what deodorant they'd wear. I was wondering if they could tell I was gay and if any of them could be gay or bisexual.

I was popular at school because of my singing and acting but when I looked in the mirror, my wicked witch inner critic said, 'You're a skinny, spotty, four-eyed, gay boy.' My inner critic who'd told me to hide my Barbie from other boys and work harder at school had two new targets: my sexuality and my appearance.

I was disappointed with what I saw. My body with which I could dance and sing and act to a professional West End standard, my body that put money in my own bank account at ten and eleven, was underperforming when compared to many of my schoolmates who were taller, more muscular, sporty or dominant in how they occupied space in the classroom, corridor, canteen, playground, in front of the school gates and walking down the street.

When my Black friends who were dark-skinned were

stopped by the police for no apparent reason, I was instructed by the police to keep moving. Was it light-skinned/mixed-race privilege? Was it my glasses? Or was it my diminutive stature compared to my friends that meant I was spared the police stop and search? I suspect it was all of the above. Flying under the radar of police suspicion felt symbolic of what I suspected about myself: I didn't stand out unless I was on stage and no boy would ever fancy me with glasses and acne.

Girls at school were starting to wear brightly coloured contacts. Many of them didn't need contact lenses to see. Black and brown girls having false blue, green and purple eyes was a trend among my peers. We weren't allowed to dye our hair unnatural colours. We weren't allowed to wear makeup or any jewellery other than a small religious symbol, but coloured contacts weren't mentioned in our school uniform dress code.

I didn't see boys wearing coloured contacts, but that didn't deter me. I had decided I wanted green contacts. They were more expensive than clear contacts, but I wasn't going to be deterred by cost. When I tried green contacts, they looked too false for my liking. I worried people might think I hated my natural brown eyes, so I went for hazel instead.

Hazel looked plausible. More natural. I felt comfortable with hazel eyes.

With hazel eyes and clearing skin, I decided to pierce my ears. The left ear was the acceptable ear for boys and men. The right ear was supposedly the gay one. I'd not come out yet, but I chose to pierce both ears to see if it caused a stir or prompted anyone to question my sexuality.

It didn't. No questions. Nothing.

You know how I came out, but I didn't know at the time how I'd come out until it happened. I thought it wouldn't happen until I'd finished high school and went off to drama school or university.

The girls I hung out with at high school were gorgeous, kind and cool, but I had no sexual appetite for them. To make matters worse, the boys I fancied patted me on the back and called me a 'player' and a 'ladies' man' because I was surrounded by popular girls. The rumours were neither denied nor confirmed.

I was popular. I didn't want my popularity to be taken away when I came out. I'd come out eventually, but my false image as a 'player' and a 'ladies' man' was comforting and didn't damage the reputations of the girls associated with me.

Within a day of me coming out as gay, the boys who'd patted me on the back started to ask me which boys I fancied. Some boys even asked if I fancied them. This scenario became a common theme through my late teens and twenties. Straight men who wanted to know how they were perceived through the eyes of a gay man. Straight men who wanted to know if my female friends fancied them.

The reality TV show *Queer Eye for the Straight Guy*, as it was called before it was rebooted as *Queer Eye*, struck such a chord because it did what good reality TV does best: it reflected real life. Straight acceptance can be othering. The gay best friend trope. A queerness in servitude of straightness. In the original format of the show, it was about being a helping hand to a straight man, so he could be more confident, dress more stylishly and generally get his shit together.

Gay men were depicted as fairy godmothers who could wave a magic wand and make things better for these unfortunate straight men. It wasn't magic. It was a haircut, some new clothes and redecorating their homes. There was some emotional piece to each episode, but the concept didn't satisfy me. If the queer eye was for the straight guy, did that mean it wasn't for me? I wanted to see the gay guy, not the straight guy, at the centre of the story. I wanted the queer eye to see me.

Queer Eye for the Straight Guy first aired in 2003, but I referred to myself as 'gay' for the entire noughties. I only started to refer to myself as 'queer' in addition to 'gay' a decade later in 2013 when Black queer photographer Ajamu X included a portrait of me alongside twenty-four others in his exhibition *Fierce: Portraits of Young Black LGBTQ+ People* at the Guildhall Art Gallery in the City of London.

Our portraits adorned the walls of the Guildhall for three months, from 1 February to 28 April 2013. I was in awe when I saw twenty-four young Black LGBTQ+ people, myself included, venerated on the walls of this Grade I-listed art gallery.

I felt seen and worthy of recognition. I stood shoulder to shoulder with my community, these young Black LGBTQ+ sitters, and the Black LGBTQ+ elders who came out to celebrate us: Ajamu and his sitters. We were part of history. We were making Black queer history. In that moment I had the grand idea I'd be included in the history books written about my generation.

'Are you allowed to say that?' asked Mummy. She'd come with me to the exhibition launch and was shocked to hear the word 'queer' used throughout the evening.

'It's all about context,' I told Mummy.

Not everyone in my generation or generations before were comfortable using the word to describe themselves or anyone else. 'Queer' has been used against some people as a slur, it still causes them pain and they don't wish to reclaim it. For others, 'queer' is an unhelpful and unclear term especially when used interchangeably with the acronym LGBTQ+.

Most of the time I feel 'gay', meaning '(of people, especially men) sexually attracted to people of the same sex'. But at the best of times, I feel 'queer', making meaning outside the boxes of gender and sexuality. Not defined by a dictionary. Defining myself from moment to moment, not a performance but an authenticity of being that doesn't have a set aesthetic and doesn't place predefined roles on myself or anyone else.

My queerness says, 'Thank you' to Ajamu X and bell hooks.

My queerness says, 'Fuck you' to 'white-supremacist capitalist patriarchy', but still wants its portraits in galleries and for you to buy my books.

My queerness is a body of work, a body of knowledge, a body politic.

My queerness sits at the intersections of race, class, gender and sexuality.

My queerness could be a game of spin the bottle, chess or backgammon.

My queerness is a child playing with a family heirloom.

My queerness is an inheritance, but what I do with it will not be dictated by older or younger generations, biological or chosen family, friends or even lovers.

My queerness is a conversation, and you have the right to reply.

My queerness believes in freedom of speech but not freedom from consequence.

My queerness is a consequence of oppression. And, no, my queerness can't cure depression.

Beautiful Thing

I'd kissed boys my age. I'd not had sex because the boys I'd kissed didn't want to do anything more. I hadn't considered the prospect of sex with an older man before I watched the TV show *Queer as Folk* in which fifteen-year-old Nathan Maloney gets with thirty-year-old Stuart Allen Jones. While Mummy watched *Queer as Folk* in the sala on full volume, I watched it on mute on my bedroom TV.

I hadn't been to Canal Street in Manchester's gay village where the show was set but I'd spent plenty of time in and around Soho, London's gay epicentre, when I was in West End musicals as a child. I took to musical theatre like a butterfly to nectar. It was a beacon of hope for boys and men like me because in the theatre we could be celebrated for our flamboyant nature. It was a safe space to be my fluttering self.

An older Jamaican relative once told me I must be careful doing musical theatre because it was 'full of batty men'. This was said with a similar screw-faced hate to that I'd seen in the barbershop. I turned to look at my cousin, Cuz, who smiled at me knowingly, conspiratorially. Cuz knew I was a batty man, and he still loved me.

Cuz was my closest cousin. I followed him to the shop more than any other cousin. Cuz had said, 'It looks like you're not Granny's favourite any more,' when I locked

71

my hair. Cuz coordinated the colour of his baseball cap with the colour of his t-shirt and his trainers. Cuz and I sneaked glasses of Baileys Irish Cream at Christmas. Cuz had told me it was okay if I was gay when he'd heard rumours about me before I was ready to come out to him and the rest of my Jamaican family. Cuz and I had little in common, but I knew he wasn't going to reject me when I came out.

Before *Queer as Folk*, the 1996 film *Beautiful Thing* about two white working-class schoolboys who fall in love against all odds was the closest to a gay fairy tale I'd ever seen. My favourite film. Based on a southeast London council estate, it didn't directly reflect me and my experience, but there was enough in the film that I could relate to, especially the single-parent households.

Beautiful Thing and *Queer as Folk* gave me courage to ask out The Redhead when I was fifteen. With no Black queer representation during my school career, I didn't consider whether any of the Black boys at my high school might be queer. The first boy I asked out was white. The eighteen-year-old hairdresser I was set up with by a school-mate after I came out was also white.

My schoolmate invited him to her place to meet me. He was her hairdresser. She thought I'd like him because he was a redhead like the boy in my drama class. The Hairdresser was tall, slim, smiley and, my schoolmate had told me, he was into Black and mixed-race guys. On paper, we were supposed to be a perfect pair.

The Hairdresser and I were left alone in the living room. It was an English living room, not a Cypriot sala, not Mummy's, not Yiayia and Bapou's. This was England and I could be free here.

The Hairdresser moved closer on the sofa and cautiously gave me a peck on the lips. This was like a match to gasoline. My dick got hard. This was it! He'd be my Stuart Allen Jones.

I mounted him hastily and shoved my tongue down his throat. As we found a rhythm with our tongues and lips, I began to gyrate my hips, I channelled the Black women I'd seen in dancehall, reggae, R&B and hip-hop music videos on MTV and The Box. His hands cupped my arse cheeks. He pulled me closer. His dick was also erect.

I wasn't supposed to have sex until I was sixteen. I was afraid – no, I was certain – once I had sex, I'd contract HIV and die of AIDS as a punishment from God for being gay. Then I'd go to hell and burn for all eternity.

I felt the flames of hell, licking, lapping, lashing the air around me. I smelled singed hair. I gasped free of The Hairdresser's mouth. My face lifted to the sky.

Is bodily gratification worth eternal damnation? No answer. More questions in quick succession. *Why is he here with you? Why can't he find someone his own age? Why an underage boy?* Still no answer.

The Hairdresser wasn't going to be my *Beautiful Thing* fairy-tale ending.

'Are you okay?' he asked.

'No,' I said. 'I've got to go.'

I left his lap and legged it without looking back, for fear of turning into a pillar of salt.

The next day my schoolmate asked why I'd left her house without saying goodbye. I didn't tell her about my fears about HIV and AIDS, hellfire and eternal damnation. I told her I didn't fancy The Hairdresser and I didn't want to see him again.

I did see him again. A decade later at an east London private members' club. The Hairdresser approached me and reminisced about that afternoon when I was fifteen and he was eighteen, recalling it as a cute teen romance. He pulled me in to dance as a familiar R&B song came on. I didn't resist and I danced closely with him. We were groin to groin once again, even though it made my skin crawl.

I felt the flames of hell all over again. We were fifteen and eighteen again, even though we were now twenty-five and twenty-eight.

How many men had I been with between fifteen and twenty-five? How many had I kissed? How many had I sucked, fucked, been sucked and fucked by?

How had I gone from 'still a virgin' to 'such a slut'? How had they gone from feeling like notches on my bedpost to skeletons in my closet? Spectres in my sphincter? How could I not remember which time was my first time?

I met men in online chatrooms. I logged in to our AOL dial-up internet at night while Mummy slept. I turned down the volume of the desktop computer so Mummy wouldn't hear the dial-up tone or the voice that said, 'Welcome to AOL' in a soft RP English accent. A voice I'd come to realise years later was that of the actress Joanna Lumley.

'Age, Sex, Location' – 'ASL' – was a typical chatroom question without a question mark. Even before I was eighteen, I'd answer, '18 Male London'. My conversations with men progressed from the chatrooms to MSN Messenger. Before I was ready to send photos, if someone asked what my skin colour was, I'd say I was the colour of a plain digestive biscuit.

When I felt comfortable enough, I'd give a man my mobile phone number and arrange to meet him after school. Sometimes at his place or sometimes in a park. I didn't have a problem with older men, though I did hope to meet someone my age, eventually. What creeped me out most was when they fetishised my youth, especially if I was wearing my school uniform when I met them.

I'd played video games since I was little, and when I got

that desktop computer, the men I met online were collect-able items. I collected their dick pics and fucked my way around the London Underground map. These men were saved in my mobile phone with their first name and their nearest tube station. Matthew Elephant and Castle. Mark King's Cross. Luke Baker Street. John Euston.

When Granny told me I favoured my father, this was a painful comparison for me. In my late teens when Mummy seemed angry at me all the time, I wondered if it was because I looked like the teenage boy she'd met at high school, the young man she'd conceived a baby with. In my late teens I was wearing the face of Mummy's high school sweetheart.

Yiayia and Bapou's was a sanctuary, a place to get away from an angry Mummy. Yiayia and Bapou sometimes shouted at each other but not at me. I spent more time at Yiayia and Bapou's after school. More time out with friends. I told Mummy I was at Yiayia and Bapou's, out with friends or working the cloakroom at one of two music venues, when I met up with older men. I wonder if I would've been a homebody if I'd not felt constantly under attack for typical teenage boy things like leaving dirty dishes in the sink, my bedroom not being tidy enough, or for looking like my dad.

Mummy cut the plug off my bedroom TV, or did she only threaten me with this? I resented it either way. 'This isn't a hotel.' 'Don't talk back to me or you can leave.' 'You're a chauvinist pig.' 'You think you're so superior.' 'You're just like your dad.'

I wasn't looking for a father figure in these older men. I had incredible uncles and my maternal grandfather, Bapou, who I adored. That's not to say I didn't have any daddy issues, but I wasn't looking for fathering from these older men. I was looking for tenderness, hoping for hugs and kisses. I was open to conversation before ejaculation.

But after I ejaculated it was a different story. My body said, 'Game Over.' I didn't want these men to touch me. I didn't want to kiss or cuddle or talk to them. I wanted to leave.

So, I left. I didn't allow them access to my body more than once. I've forgotten their faces and their real names, but I've not forgotten how I felt: ashamed.

I went from bad sex to bad sex. Sex in gay saunas. Sex in secret, in parks and graveyards, in parked cars and moving trains, in toilets, in stairwells and garages. I rarely used condoms despite knowing I should. I was certain I'd test positive for HIV every time I visited a sexual health clinic. I was playing STI Bingo or perhaps Russian roulette, HIV the single round in the revolver. The stigma of the time combined with my own fear and shame and became an inner tricolour: the flag of me that only I could see.

In the arms of The Hairdresser, I was devastated that in the decade from fifteen to twenty-five I'd not found my fairy-tale ending. The Hairdresser represented every man I'd kissed, fucked or dated and ultimately not ended up with. When the R&B song ended, I told him it was good to see him again. He asked for my number, and I gave it to him without thinking and returned to my group of friends who were used to me slipping away with redheaded men.

The Hairdresser would message me sporadically over the subsequent years to say he was thinking of me, tell me how sexy I had grown up to be, ask me to come to his flat to hang out. He became one of several men with whom I entertained the idea of something happening again, even though I wasn't interested. Late at night, I'd respond and give these men false hope that we might reunite.

I'd ask them to describe what they'd like to do if we

were together. I'd ask them to send me photos of their dick, their arse or a full naked body shot. I'd also send dick, arse and full naked body shots on request. Old photos. *Blue Peter* style: 'Here's one I made earlier.'

I wouldn't allow access to my body as it was in the moment. Their photos could've been old photos too. I didn't care about that. Or them. I'd send and receive messages of this nature to multiple men at once. Once I'd cum on my own in my bedroom, I'd put down my mobile phone and clean myself up. Relieved for a while, I'd ghost them. I'd ignore messages from them for days, weeks or months until I felt lonely again.

When I ghosted someone, it was because I'd decided to drop the character I was playing in our shared story. I dropped my mask; I dropped the persona or alter ego I'd created to hide behind to interact with them. I had an unlimited number of personas, one for every man I met or messaged. While I didn't get any leading roles in West End musicals, I sure knew how to lead men on.

I was a player, of more than video games, but not the ladies' man schoolmates once thought me to be. I ghosted men easily because no one knew the real me. The person they knew was as changeable as a profile picture or avatar. I discarded my masks like the hollow tracing-paper skin shed by my pet snake Ben. Then, I'd slither away from them.

I was a snake that couldn't be charmed. I didn't care how these men felt. I didn't care if they thought this late-night talking could be leading somewhere. Once I'd decided a man wasn't my Prince Charming, I'd moonwalk out of his life at supersonic speed, and he wouldn't have a fighting chance of catching me.

Through Their Eyes

Mummy said I should wear a suit. The royal crest on my gilded invite from Queen Elizabeth II to attend the poets' reception at Buckingham Palace on 19 November 2013 suggested a formal dress code. I didn't own a suit, so I bought a cut-price navy blue designer suit from TK Maxx for the occasion. I'd figured the suit was a sound investment because I'd be able to wear it again at my graduation when I completed the Writer/Teacher master's degree I was doing part-time at Goldsmiths, University of London. Alongside this, I was working part-time as a spoken word educator in an east London secondary school. I was a busy boy back then.

I'd had many other day jobs that allowed me to do spoken word poetry in the evenings. One of my day jobs had been as an employment and training adviser in west London. Mummy got me the job and was my line manager. I was a model employee. I had to be. I didn't want to disappoint or embarrass Mummy.

I gave employment and training advice to NEET – Not in Employment, Education or Training – young people. My work attire was a smart casual halfway house. Some days: jeans with a shirt; other days: trousers with a t-shirt. I didn't wear a suit because I didn't own a suit, but I didn't wear a tracksuit because I'd look like one of my NEET clients if I wore a tracksuit.

It felt absurd for me – a twentysomething spoken word poet who worked in his mum's office and lived in her house rent-free – to be giving advice to other young people. But my NEET clients listened to me and seemed to respect me because I was closer to their age than many of the other staff in the office. This job was a stopgap for me, but I knew most of the NEET clients didn't have the parental support I had.

I tried to broaden their horizons. The boys wanted to join the army, and the girls wanted to do childcare or hair and beauty. I'd challenge this social conditioning and float other ideas. I tried to disabuse them of their beliefs that they had limited options because of their current level of education or overall lack of cultural capital. While I understood they wanted to start making money as soon as possible, I wanted them to consider how their prospects and earning potential could be improved and increased by conventional or vocational education. Somewhere in my academic career I'd picked up the idea that 'the more you learn, the more you earn', a quote attributed to American business magnate, investor and philanthropist Warren Buffett. I don't know why I, a young Black British man, was quoting corporate America to boys who wanted to be soldiers and girls who wanted to be hairdressers. I saw myself through their eyes, as someone who looked familiar, like a friend, sibling, cousin or neighbour, but sounded out of touch with their surroundings and present reality. Ultimately it was their decision to make and their futures.

I didn't feel much pressure to make decisions about my future in my twenties because I could live with Mummy rent-free. Since I'd moved back to Mummy's in London after three years at university in Brighton, she didn't yell at me like she used to, and her critical comments didn't sting me like they used to. It didn't feel unusual for me to be living at Mummy's in my twenties. Cypriot Uncle lived at Yiayia and Bapou's and my dad lived at Granny's.

'Do what makes you happy,' was still Mummy's main advice for me. Classic Mummy wisdom!

As a twentysomething, I still didn't know what would make me happy.

So, I went with the flow, doing day jobs that suited me while doing spoken word poetry in the evenings.

Most of the poets around me didn't have the parental support I had either. Not only financial but moral support. Mummy came to my spoken word poetry performances and sat in the front row. When I began to produce and host these events, Mummy would work the door: taking money and ticking names off the guest list. She was invaluable to my growth as a spoken word poet, event host and producer. I don't remember if I asked her or if she volunteered for this role, but I do remember knowing I could rely on her and noticing how much better we got on outside her house.

'I like helping you,' she'd say, 'and I've got my magazines to read if I get bored of the poetry.'

Mummy was impressed when I was in the office giving advice to NEET clients or producing and hosting spoken word poetry events, but she was thoroughly unimpressed if I left dirty dishes in the sink at home. Mummy's love felt unconditional, but her respect felt contingent on me being impressive or at least clean and tidy. I was an impressive performer. I was an impressive event host and producer. I was an impressive employment and training adviser. And I knew, without a shadow of a doubt, I was an impressive spoken word educator. However, I wasn't as confident about my own writing. My inner critic loomed large when I sat down to write or stepped up to perform.

Although I'd used words like 'revolution' in the poems I'd written in my teens and referred to myself as a 'King' who would 'reclaim my throne'. I no longer thought of my poems as literal rallying cries. I wasn't trying to bring down the monarchy. I wasn't a republican or a royalist. I wasn't anti-establishment. I wasn't trying hard enough, according to my inner critic.

I'd attended receptions at London's City Hall and 10 Downing Street and shaken hands with Gordon Brown, Boris Johnson and David Cameron. This was not a matter of pride or shame for me, just a matter of fact. I'd been part of organisations doing work these leaders acknowledged with canapés and a handshake photo opportunity. At first, I was invited as an inspirational young person and later I was invited as someone who was an inspiration to young people. The shift happened when I turned twenty-five and was no longer considered young in the eyes of arts organisations, youth initiatives and funding bodies.

The invite to Buckingham Palace seemed to be in the vein of invites to City Hall and 10 Downing Street: shake a hand, smile for photos, eat the free food. I knew placing my body before the queen and shaking her hand could be seen as an endorsement for the monarchy, but it didn't seem logical to accept invitations to meet a London mayor and two prime ministers and decline an invitation to meet the queen. If the UK was a video game, the queen was the Big Boss.

I was used to seeing the queen's face on bank notes, coins and stamps. Mummy watched the Queen's Speech on TV on Christmas Day. The queen had sat on the throne since long before Mummy was born. The queen had ruled over Cyprus and Jamaica when they were British crown colonies until 1960 and 1962, respectively. I was unsure if I'd feel angry or amazed when I stood face to face with the queen. She was not only Queen of the UK and other Commonwealth realms, but she was also the head of the

Church of England into which I had been baptised and confirmed at fifteen.

I remembered feeling excited about the royal family when I was at my C of E primary school in the Royal Borough of Kensington and Chelsea. While my school wasn't a private school, being in a royal borough felt special. I felt some proximity to royalty when a royal helicopter landed during school sports day at the paddock owned by Kensington Palace. I wouldn't have been surprised if I'd felt a similar excitement meeting the queen as I had as a little boy leaving my lane, abandoning an egg and spoon race, to wave at a royal helicopter.

We lined up and, one by one, the queen shook our hands. When my turn came to meet the monarch, to touch royalty, I looked the queen in the eye and saw Yiayia. The queen looked like my maternal grandmother had been given a *Queer Eye* makeover. She looked fabulous, this superimposed Queen Yiayia/Yiayia Queen, in my imagination. She wore a lavender lace skirt suit with a gold brooch, a black handbag and black court shoes. It was over in a flash, like when I met Michael Jackson.

Then, Carol Ann Duffy spoke as the Poet Laureate of the UK, as did John Agard as the recipient of the queen's gold medal for poetry. It was quite something to see an Openly Lesbian Poet Laureate and a Black Caribbean poet acknowledged and celebrated at Buckingham Palace. Quite something indeed.

But the most exciting part of the poets' reception for me was when I met the actress, and self-proclaimed poetry lover, Joanna Lumley. I'd grown up watching her on TV as the iconic Patsy Stone in *Absolutely Fabulous*.

Ab Fab was one of the most beloved TV shows for queer people of my generation, giving LGBTQ+ representation across five seasons from 1992 to 2003. In person, Joanna reminded me of Jodie Harsh until I realised that was the wrong way round: Jodie would've been inspired by Patsy.

Patsy was a firm favourite for drag queens to emulate and pay homage to, like Moira Rose in *Schitt's Creek* is today. Patsy's blonde beehive hairdo and striking red lipstick, power dressing, chain smoking and champagne lunches, along with her fierce temper, are just a few of the reasons she's an icon. She was bold and beautiful, a glam-azon who inspired people of all genders.

Joanna was warm, gently spoken, graceful, and generous with the attention she showed me. She seemed genuinely interested in speaking with me about poetry. I couldn't help but expect an outburst from her TV character, the potty-mouthed powerhouse, Patsy Stone.

In my mind I could hear Patsy's pointed and pernicious tone as she called her best friend's daughter a 'bitch troll from hell'. Joanna spoke nothing like Patsy. It took me a moment to remember why Joanna's natural voice was already familiar.

'Welcome to AOL.'

The desktop computer. The dial-up internet. The men in online chatrooms.

This was my second time in the same building as Joanna. Earlier that year I'd performed a poem at a fundraising gala at the Lyric Hammersmith where she was guest of honour. I reminded her of this when I said hello at Buckingham Palace, and she said she remembered my performance. I boldly asked if I could send her a copy of my debut poetry collection, *I Am Nobody's Nigger*.

'I would love that!' Joanna said.

The use of the n-word in my book's title had prompted another 'Are you allowed to do that?' line of questioning from Mummy. My answer to Mummy this time hadn't been as clear as it had been for the word 'queer'. I'd told Mummy that my publisher thought this was the obvious (and only) book title on the table. Since I'd wanted that title as well, I hadn't asked if my book deal depended on this. I don't think it would've been a deal-breaker. I did receive criticism for the book's title, but it was outweighed by praise for the poems.

After I sent Joanna a copy, she sent me an email to tell me my 'wonderful collection of poems' was 'powerful stuff, and so moving and heart-breaking'. She went on to name which poems she was 'struck by'. She said she loved reading poetry and always kept some by her bedside, which is where my book currently was. She closed her email by thanking me and wishing me a Merry Christmas and a Happy New Year.

I saw myself through her eyes. My poetry was 'wonderful'. My poetry was 'powerful stuff'. My poetry was good enough to make a positive impression on an icon like Joanna.

Meeting the queen was certainly noteworthy but making this connection with Joanna through poetry meant more to me than any royal recognition. I'm glad my phone was locked away on arrival at Buckingham Palace. If I'd had my phone on me, this delightful meeting might have turned into something as trivial as a selfie with her.

Meeting Joanna was a fairy-tale moment in a palace. This hadn't been like meeting Gwen Stefani years earlier when I worked at Shepherd's Bush Empire, I wasn't simply starstruck by Joanna, I felt something bigger and warmer. I was Cinderella meeting my fairy godmother. Instead of granting wishes or a *Queer Eye* style makeover, Joanna helped me believe in myself and see that I already had the magic I needed to succeed. I saw myself through her eyes, as someone who had written a 'wonderful collection of poems'.

I'd received words of affirmation from notable people

before Joanna, including one of my early influences, Benjamin Zephaniah: 'Dean Atta's poetry is as honest as truth itself. He follows no trend, he seeks no favours, this is him. He is his biggest influence.' I didn't see myself that way; I brushed off Benjamin's high praise as hyperbole at the time because he'd told me I was ready to publish my debut poetry collection, when other older writers had warned me that my manuscript wasn't ready to be published, and I'd felt torn about who to listen to.

I'd first met Benjamin four years earlier in 2009 at a SLAMbassadors spoken word poetry event at Rich Mix in east London. SLAMbassadors was a young people's poetry slam organised by Joelle Taylor for the Poetry Society. Benjamin was a guest performer. At the end of the event, I took a deep breath, puffed up my chest, strutted towards Benjamin and presented him with a CD of some of my spoken word poems.

I was bold like this in my twenties. I was the support act, with a spoken word poetry set, for English R&B and soul singer Terri Walker at the Jazz Café in Camden, because I wrote to her and asked if I could be. When Ursula Rucker came to London from America, I went to her show to introduce myself to her, and we stayed in touch online.

I messaged Benjamin on MySpace a few weeks later to check if he'd listened to it.

He had!

Benjamin wrote back with praise and invited me to keep sending him my poems. I did. And I didn't stop until he told me I had enough poems for a collection.

When I chose a publisher for my debut poetry collection, Benjamin looked over my contract – because I didn't have an agent back then – and gave me this endorsement for the front cover: 'Love your eyes over these words of truth. You will be uplifted.' I couldn't see myself through

Benjamin's eyes. Soon after publication I felt I'd made a mistake by making my debut too soon.

For as long as I can remember, my inner critic has had it in for me like a school bully homing in on my insecurities, like a punishing schoolteacher admonishing me for my spelling mistakes. My inner critic kicks me when I'm down, and cuts short all celebration, like Patsy Stone. But since the brief meeting with – and an affirming email from – Joanna, my inner critic has been rivalled by an inner cheerleader who sees the good in me, an inner cheerleader with a soft RP voice remarkably similar to that of my fairy godmother, Joanna Lumley.

I have long wondered why Benjamin's thoughtful Brummie accent didn't become the voice of my inner cheerleader. I reckon it has something to do with the grand occasion of my meeting Joanna and the fact that I haven't seen her since, whereas Benjamin remained present in my life for a long time – in word and deed. Over the years I saw Benjamin often and spoke to him about many things – not only poetry and publishing but the state of the nation, the state of the world and, of course, veganism.

When I became vegan at thirty in 2015, Benjamin was pleased – so pleased in fact that I didn't have the heart to tell him I stopped being vegan after two years. Benjamin had been drug-free, teetotal and vegan since he was thirty. I wanted to hold on to our vegan connection because – besides dyslexia, typewriters, our Jamaican heritage and love of Bob Marley – our lives were so different. Benjamin wouldn't have gone to Buckingham Palace to meet the queen; in 2003 Benjamin had declined an OBE.

When I expressed my anxiety to Benjamin about turning thirty, he told me he'd spent his thirtieth birthday locked up in a police station – this comparison brought my life into sharp focus and forced me to face my relative privilege and freedom. I remembered his poem 'Dis Policeman Keeps on Kicking Me To Death', a poem that was two years older than me. I looked up to Benjamin long before he became my friend and mentor. Benjamin has been a guiding light in my life, a role model, a respected elder, and now he is a beloved ancestor. And, at the tail end of my thirties, I'm starting to see myself the way he saw me.

VOICE

A Voice From Nowhere

I saw myself in Charlie from Roald Dahl's *Charlie and the Chocolate Factory*. Not only because I loved chocolate. Something about him felt familiar. In a 2017 BBC documentary Roald Dahl's widow, Liccy Dahl, said, 'His first Charlie that he wrote about was a little black boy.' I felt a flutter in my belly at the idea that Charlie could've been a Black boy.

Like Charlie, my family was poor but rich in love. That's how I felt as a child. My Cypriot grandparents had no central heating but did have an electric two-bar heater in the sala that only came on in the dead of winter. I didn't share a bed with my grandparents, like Charlie, but bed was the warmest place in their London house. I needed several blankets on top of my duvet on winter nights at Yiayia and Bapou's.

'Théleis tsái?' Yiayia would offer me another cup of tea before I'd had a chance to finish the last.

When I watched TV with Yiayia and Bapou, I mimicked Bapou's chain-smoking by blowing breath into the cold air of their unheated sala. Even though it was no laughing matter, I mimicked Bapou's chronic cough and raspy voice, his body's distress. I believed 'Smoking Kills' long before they put the words on the packet. I thought Bapou might drop dead at any moment. This gallows humour helped me to cope. The walls of the sala were stained yellow by tobacco smoke. I believed Bapou's lungs were similarly stained, and his days were numbered. He would soon be six feet under.

Bapou had one foot in the grave from my point of view. But Bapou wasn't as curmudgeonly as Victor Meldrew. Bapou kept most of his quips and snipes to himself, but you could see them firing from his eyes at Yiayia, at Mummy and her siblings. But Bapou's deep-seated hostility was never directed towards me.

I believed Yiayia and Bapou were poor. Having been told by Mummy that she and I were homeless for the first year of my life, without an explanation, I believed the addition of me meant there were too many mouths to feed.

Mummy had told Yiayia and Bapou she was pregnant with me at seventeen; they kicked her out for being pregnant out of wedlock and by a Black man. And so, Mummy and I were homeless for the first year of my life. We were allocated a room in a B&B, then moved to a council flat with water leaking through the ceiling from the upstairs neighbours. Mummy said the council kept redecorating the walls to hide the fact that the damp proof course had failed.

We were moved somewhere suitable before Little Sis was born when I was eight. We were a single parent household with two children by two different dads. Little Sis saw her dad every other Sunday, while I only saw my dad every so often if he came out of his bedroom when I visited Granny's.

Yiayia and Bapou were providing some childcare and financial support by this point. I dreamed of becoming 'rich' when I grew up because I was sure there wasn't enough money in my Cypriot family. Whereas my Jamaican family had Jamaican Uncle who could support them all, I didn't see signs of wealth in my Cypriot family. I thought one day

I might have to support them all. My acting career would be my golden ticket.

I had no idea that Bapou wasn't poor, he was frugal. I had no idea he'd kicked Mummy out of his London house and punitively withheld his financial support because he didn't support her decision to have me. And when Mummy told me these things, it felt like she was being vengeful.

I couldn't unlove Yiayia and Bapou. I couldn't resent them on Mummy's behalf. Bapou had been kind to me for as long as I could remember. I couldn't remember being a homeless one-year-old, but once Mummy had told me about it, I couldn't forget it. I was afraid we would somehow be made homeless again.

When I was seven, I wasn't aware of class in a meaningful way. My primary school was in the Royal Borough of Kensington and Chelsea, the same borough as the 547-room Kensington Palace and the same borough where the 24-storey Grenfell Tower block stood before the tragic fire of 14 June 2017, which killed seventy-two people.

Some of my friends lived in flats in tower blocks like Grenfell and others lived in four-storey houses and had a dedicated playroom aside from their bedroom, while others lived in two-bedroom houses like me, and a few lived in embassies because their parents were diplomats from other countries. As well as in each other's homes, we had play-dates in Holland Park and Kensington Gardens. We went to the cinema at Whiteleys shopping centre and bowling and ice skating in Bayswater. I have three standout one-off memories from that time: going sailing and someone yelling 'man the rigging' and having to put my whole body into pulling a rope, that royal helicopter landing during my egg and spoon race during school sports day at the paddock owned by Kensington Palace and going to my first ballet at the Royal Albert Hall.

As we got older, the differences between my schoolmates became clearer; when we'd hang out at Portobello Road Market, some of us had money to spend and others didn't. I didn't consider whose family owned their house or flat. I didn't know anything about home ownership versus renting. I didn't know about the class system. I didn't know that some of my friends' families were working class, others were middle class, and some may have been obscenely wealthy. The distinction I made at seven was between having a home and being homeless.

I had a homeless friend I used to chat to before and after primary school for some years. He was a white man who sold the *Big Issue* magazine on the high street of my primary school. It took a while for him to be housed. He stayed in hostels and temporary accommodation before getting his own place. He had a history of addiction and was estranged from his family.

Mummy would buy the *Big Issue* from him each week, but she'd also hand me coins to give him every day. It didn't feel like a handout. I sat and spoke with him every day after school. I'd show him things I'd made in class such as the papier-mâché mask adorned with an Aztec-inspired design: a turquoise mosaic of blue and green pieces of paper and a permanent white smile. I'd tell him when I'd received a good grade for a piece of schoolwork, and he'd congratulate and celebrate with me. I hope he enjoyed our chats. There were no male teachers in primary school, so he was one of the few men outside my family I had one-to-one time with.

I remember him as a friend.

Now I'm more critical of this dynamic, wondering if when we gave him money, we paid for him to be friendly to us. I don't know. What matters most is how it felt. This man was my friend. I looked forward to seeing him every day.

My most striking memory of the time I spent with him was when he had superglued a 50-pence piece to the pavement a few feet in front of where he sat. I sat with him and watched people in business attire and designer clothes stop in their tracks, swoop down like magpies, placing their briefcases or bulging shopping bags on the ground to attempt to pick up this silver-coloured coin. When they couldn't get a grip of it with their fingers, some would stand and try to kick it free of the pavement with the toe or heel of their shoe. The *Big Issue* Man and I giggled at their extreme exertion of energy. There's nothing to say these people wouldn't have given the 50-pence coin to The *Big Issue* Man. However, when he said, *Big Issue*, and they seemed to notice him for the first time, they scooped up their belongings and scurried away.

I moved through primary school, not only up the year groups but also from the small playground to the long playground and finally to the big playground. The *Big Issue* Man was housed and got another job on a market stall near to my Saturday stage school. I went from seeing him Monday to Friday to only once a week after my Saturday singing, dance and drama classes. He was in his element standing tall on the market stall. His voice boomed out with his market trader patter, of prices and special offers; he was no longer sat on the ground almost invisible, no longer a voice from nowhere.

The *Big Issue* Man's journey from homelessness to market stall trader felt Dickensian in nature. I thought about him a lot when I performed in *Oliver!* at the London Palladium at ten and eleven. I loaned my unbroken voice to fictional characters, but I channelled a very real and important person in my life: my friend The *Big Issue* Man.

Mummy knew lots of people like The *Big Issue* Man, who she'd go out of her way to talk to: market stall traders, shop keepers, schoolteachers and parents at my primary school and Saturday stage school, people at church and around our neighbourhood. And yet she wouldn't answer the house-phone when it rang or the door when someone knocked.

Before Little Sis was born, Mummy took naps when we got home, and I'd watch cartoons, play with my toys and video games, or make my magazine styled after the *Big Issue* using the old typewriter Mummy had given me. I'd write and illustrate my magazine in a four-step process. One, with a letter stencil I wrote the title, *DEAN'S MAGAZINE*, in block capitals. Two, I drew boxes where the pictures would go, so I could type around them. Three, I loaded the titled and formatted A4 sheet of paper into the typewriter and I'd make up the story as I typed it. Four, I drew pictures on a separate piece of paper, cut them out and stuck them into the empty box spaces I'd left for them. Magazine complete.

I reckon I wrote my petition against our 'yucky' school lunches on this typewriter after school when Mummy was napping. There were other issues I could've launched a petition about: toilet rolls at school that made it feel like you were wiping your bum with tracing paper or the jacket-stealing ghost in the cloakroom. But school lunches were my priority.

I took the petition into school the next day. Mummy said she had no knowledge of it until she was summoned by The Headteacher. Mummy tells me that The Headteacher told her she was impressed with me but appalled at the number of spelling mistakes in the petition. Even though this was noticed at age seven, I didn't get a dyslexia diagnosis until I was eighteen.

At age seven, I was gathered in the school hall with every child who'd signed the petition. The Headteacher had written out the correct spelling of every word I'd spelled incorrectly in the petition. She said that, while these mistakes had been made by me, everyone who signed the petition had become responsible for them by signing without first checking what they'd signed up to. Everyone had to write the correct spelling of each word out ten times before they would be dismissed to have their lunch. My face was red with embarrassment, indignation and anger: the substance of the petition had been dismissed because I'd spelled some words wrong. My attempt to speak truth to power was met with punishment. This punishment was wrong.

This was the only time I was in trouble with The Headteacher. My past misdemeanours had been minor: I'd collected all the paper clips I could find in my classroom and linked them into a chain which I kept in my bookbag drawer: a growing secret snake I kept hidden, years before I had my real pet snake Ben. Every time my class teacher replenished our paper clip stock, I'd pilfer some and add them to my ever-growing paper clip chain. At the end of term when my class teacher found the paper clip chain coiled in my bookbag drawer like a snake in its hide, she held it up, one paper clip between her thumb and index finger, and let the chain uncoil and trail to the ground. It was twice as tall as me. I wouldn't have known this without her assistance. I was impressed with how it had grown. It was the end of term anyway, so I was ready to call it quits. I didn't need to take home this snake of paper clips. I had everything I needed at home: toys, video games, a bike, rollerblades, a skateboard and a typewriter.

'Sorry,' I said, 'I promise I won't steal again.'

Did I ever break this promise? Yes, I did. But I knew what my class teacher wanted to hear. I didn't think I'd stolen the paper clips. I'd repurposed them. I'd kept them to myself. I'd hidden them. But I hadn't stolen them yet.

Most likely I was going to take the paper clip chain home that end of term. But we'll never know for sure.

My class teacher forgave me for pilfering paper clips, while The Headteacher humiliated me for the petition. I received no indication my complaint about school dinners had been taken seriously despite Mummy telling me The Headteacher had said she was impressed. Instead, The Headteacher used my spelling mistakes to shame me. I didn't hate The Headteacher for this. I turned my negative feelings inwards. They emboldened my inner critic to demand nothing less than perfection when it came to my writing and my life.

This was a tall order for an as-yet-undiagnosed dyslexic child who didn't know why he made so many mistakes, who couldn't see his mistakes, who didn't yet have that desktop computer with a word processor and spellcheck, who relied on the *Oxford English Dictionary* and Tipp-Ex to seek and hide his mistakes.

I saw my primary school headteacher some years later. I was a high school student. She was the neighbour of one of Mummy's work colleagues. Mummy and I were sat out in her work colleague's garden drinking ice-cold drinks on a summer's day. The wooden fences were waist height. Rows of manicured lawns and flowerbeds. Wooden furniture, not the white plastic garden chairs I was familiar with. The Headteacher came out to tend to her roses. I thought of Bapou in his northwest London garden tending to his roses.

'Hello, Dean!' The Headteacher beamed with a smile the likes of which I'd not seen on her face before, her RP voice softer than I remembered. As I stood to greet her across the garden fence, I was taller. I remembered how The Headteacher used to tower over me, making me feel small. Standing in her garden in her floral summer dress she looked like a lovely little older lady, like Yiayia and not an all-powerful headteacher with the ability to shame and silence me.

It was heartening to see The Headteacher this one last time in a different context; it softened my mental image of her. I didn't know what her life consisted of beyond the role she'd played in mine as the ultimate disciplinarian. Seeing her in that garden in her summer dress, she was no longer limited to a one-dimensional caricature in my mind.

I Said, 'I Love You'

I said 'I love you' to The Doctor within the first month of meeting him in 2018. Much to his astonishment, I said that first 'I love you' during sex. He was on his back with his legs over my shoulders as I rooted into him.

The Doctor didn't say anything back. I kissed him and I carried on kissing and fucking him until we both came. It felt amazing to tell him I loved him. I didn't need him to say it back to me in that moment, I was confident he would eventually love me in return. I'd had enough sex and been on enough dates to know The Doctor and I were compatible in all the ways that mattered.

The Doctor had driven us down from London early that morning to go for a walk along the Devil's Dyke valley on the South Downs in Sussex. Even though I'd lived in Brighton for university and worked in and around Brighton and Sussex since, I'd not been to Devil's Dyke. Raves in the woods around campus and meditating on the pebble beach were the closest I got to nature during my three years there.

The Doctor laughed at my rush of excitement as I skipped along, and we descended into the 100-metre-deep V-shaped grassy valley. Walking through that valley for the first time, I felt cradled in Mother Nature's elbow. I felt small in the best way possible.

'It's like a Brontosaurus is going to appear over there or a pterodactyl is going to fly over us,' I said, as I pointed ahead and above like hour and minute hands that read three o'clock.

I felt a flutter in my belly as my body clock wound back. I felt like the eight-year-old boy watching *Jurassic Park* for the first time in the cinema in 1993, something The Doctor wouldn't have done because he was only one when it was released. The Doctor laughed and snapped a photo of me with his Nikon DSLR camera. He took photos of me and the landscape all day. And all day I felt love approaching like the footsteps of a Tyrannosaurus rex.

Once we'd checked into our holiday B&B attic room above a pub, we sat on the chaise longue at the foot of our bed, and The Doctor showed me his photos of the day. I knew we were making memories. I couldn't help but think of the B&B Mummy and I lived in for the first year of my life. I knew this would be the first year of many with The Doctor if we were lucky.

I felt another flutter in my belly. I'd not felt so seen, so literally seen, and worthy of attention since Ajamu X had included me in his exhibition. I looked at the photos The Doctor had taken of me in the landscape of Devil's Dyke. I looked happier than I'd seen myself for years.

In that moment, I fell in love with The Doctor, his camera and his hazel eyes behind the lens. He'd captured something I'd not seen in myself for a long time. Not only did I feel seen by The Doctor I felt in safe hands and in good heart in his company. And after we'd had sex, I slept soundly.

As day follows night, when a seagull squawked a wake-up call and I opened my eyes to the sleeping face of The Doctor, when with the index finger of my left hand I stroked his caterpillar eyebrows, one and two, and with the same finger I sloped the mountain of his nose, I knew I was in love. It wasn't our first time waking up together, we'd spent the night in each other's bedrooms, but it was our first time waking up together somewhere new.

When we had sex that morning I said, 'I love you', which meant, 'I choose you', which also meant, 'I love how you make me feel. I love how you make me feel seen. I love how you've shown me somewhere new. I love Devil's Dyke. I love the valley between your arse cheeks. I love having sex with you. I love how free I feel with you. I love myself when I'm with you.'

I could've said, 'I want to look into your hazel eyes for the rest of our lives.'

I could've said, 'I can see myself loving you.'

I could've said, 'One day I will love you.'

Instead, I said, 'I love you.'

And it was true.

When I went to get dressed that morning, I saw the fresh clothes I'd packed were black, like yesterday's clothes on the floor.

'Bapou! Agápi mou.'

I'd forgotten I was mourning the death of my maternal grandfather, Bapou. What was meant to be forty days and nights wearing black had become many months for me. For one day and night I'd felt all right. The returning grief felt familiar.

Grief had made a home of me. It could come and go as it pleased. It returned that morning to find another house-mate took up a little more space than before. Love had lived here first. Love welcomed grief home with open arms. Grief was relieved for the company.

Sometimes I call The Doctor 'agápi mou', 'my love' in Greek. Even though he doesn't speak Greek. Greek is my love language. The language of my maternal grandparents. Some days my love resists translation.

A Voice Like That

'If I had a voice like that, I'd sing all the time,' I said.

The Doctor and I were doing karaoke one evening on a holiday in Italy, a holiday during which we practised yoga most mornings and swam in the sea or a lake every day. He sang a duet on his own: 'Guilty' by Barbra Streisand and Barry Gibb. He sang on his own not only because I didn't know the song but because he was ready to shine. He was pitch-perfect and characterised both parts with panache. I was gobsmacked. It felt like I was being pranked, like a professional singer was going to appear from the wings and reveal they were the one singing.

I fell even more in love with him, something I didn't know was possible because I thought I was already all the way in. I'd not seen The Doctor in performance mode other than when he practised clarinet and guitar at home. I found it sexy that he had this hidden skill. I knew him well, but he could surprise me still. I'd been with The Doctor for years, and it felt like he'd been keeping this sexy secret from me.

I thought of the two redheaded R&B singers I'd dated. The flipside of admiration for your partner is it can create a false sense of rivalry. Comparison is the thief of joy.

In an attempt to match The Doctor's performance, my karaoke song was a mock duet, at least that's how it was presented in the music video in which Lauryn Hill performs as two versions of herself, one singing and one rapping 'Doo Wop (That Thing)'. I didn't know the words as well as I thought I did. I felt embarrassed by my performance if you could even call it that.

In my mind I rewind to the noughties with albums by Craig David, D'Angelo, Erykah Badu, Lauryn Hill and The Roots on repeat on my Sony Discman portable CD player. I had albums by Britney Spears and the Spice Girls as well, but I was mostly into R&B. My ABC of female R&B singers was Aaliyah, Brandy and Mariah Carey. I remembered Christina Aguilera and Justin Timberlake sitting pretty in the sweet spot of R&B/pop and the rise of Destiny's Child with lead singer Beyoncé the standout star of the group.

I remembered why I didn't sing, rap or do karaoke often: I didn't think I had the voice, confidence or wild abandon required to enjoy it; it reminded me that I wasn't a star; it wasn't fun for me to be mediocre at singing or rapping – art forms I love and admire above most others.

The Miseducation Of Lauryn Hill is a masterpiece. That Lauryn went on to have four children with one of Bob Marley's sons made perfect sense to me. Not only is Lauryn a queen in my eyes, but she is music royalty. Lauryn also writes poetry. Her spoken word poetry performance 'Motives and Thoughts' on season five episode one of HBO's *Def Poetry Jam* spurred me on to raid the TV show's back catalogue on YouTube, where I saw my beloved Ursula Rucker and was introduced to other incredible spoken word poets such as Saul Williams and The Last Poets.

Def Poetry Jam was a spoken word poetry show, hosted by American rapper, singer, songwriter and actor, Mos Def, that aired on HBO between 2002 and 2007. I can't say what year I was made wise to its presence online, but it must've been after February 2005 when YouTube launched. I saw music artists such as Mos Def and Erykah Badu in a new light. Stripped back and unaccompanied. They were into the thing I knew how to do, something I did to a high standard.

I saw UK-based poets on *Def Poetry Jam*, people I'd met, such as Floetry, Jonzi D, Linton Kwesi Johnson and Zena Edwards. This showed me the potential for Black British spoken word poetry to be a big deal internationally and made real the possibility for my voice to be heard on that scale. With examples like Floetry, Jonzi, Linton and Zena, I dared to dream my voice, my words, would be heard internationally through the medium of spoken word poetry.

Mummy changed tack in her approach to my career: she took a break from telling me to do what makes me happy and tried to convince me I could be the next Craig David. This reminded me of Secret Crush comparing me to Will Smith. I wondered why Mummy chose Craig David as an example rather than George Michael or Peter Andre, who were both British Cypriots.

George Michael publicly came out in 1998, after an undercover policeman arrested him for engaging in a lewd act in a public toilet in Los Angeles. I'd not been to L.A., but I'd had plenty of sex in public toilets. I didn't tell Mummy this. I told Mummy that I didn't sing any more and my poems were nothing like Craig David's songs.

Fast-forward to 2012 when I arrived at the Southampton home studio of Mark Hill aka Artful, one half of the production duo Artful Dodger who co-wrote and produced Craig David's debut album *Born To Do It*. Artful had just co-written a song with Ed Sheeran. I'd met Ed a few times – I'd booked him to perform at one of the music and poetry nights I hosted, and I bumped into him at other events and at an east London private members' club that was popular with the entertainment industry – but Artful and I weren't introduced by Ed. I was introduced to Artful by Georgia Lewis Anderson, a presenter on SB.TV, a British music media company and YouTube channel founded by Jamal Edwards, on which the video for my poem 'I Am Nobody's Nigger' – directed and produced by Paris Zarcilla – had gone viral.

I'd found myself in Mummy's *Top of the Pops* dream for me. It hadn't happened randomly. Mummy's belief in me planted a seed that grew inside me and bloomed into my studio session with Artful. He'd named his independent label Workhouse Records: another homage to Charles Dickens's *Oliver Twist*. Maybe this had been destined since I'd appeared in those West End productions of *Oliver!* at ten and eleven. Several children I'd performed alongside as a child too had grown up to be famous Hollywood actors, TV personalities and pop stars – Tom Fletcher, Jamie Bell and Sheridan Smith spring to mind. These names aren't claims to fame or attempts to garner reflected glory for my story. These names serve to contextualise my proximity to people who had achieved mainstream success.

As an adult I'd recorded with incredible musicians and music producers, but none of my songs felt authentic despite the talent of my collaborators – Ayanna Witter-Johnson, Renell Shaw and Yussef Dayes to name a few. I made regular visits to the northwest London home studio of Kevin Mark Trail, a collaborator of Mike Skinner aka The Streets. My issue was that I didn't have a clear vision for my musical projects. I loved the concept albums of The Streets, but I didn't yet have the discipline to stay with one storyline for a long time. I flitted between collaborators and home studios like I'd flitted between friend groups at high school. Making music wasn't my dream, being a writer was. Music was something Mummy suggested, and I chose to run with it. My three spoken word poetry EPs – *Reason & Rhyme*, *Missing Piece* and *Love or Money* – were in keeping with the poetry pamphlets, zines and CDs of my peers. They were testing grounds for new ideas. They were the building blocks of our arts practice and careers.

In the studio with Artful, I was role-playing being a musician when I knew deep down that I wasn't one. I was a poet at heart. While I'd loved performing with live bands at events like REMEDY, Tongue Fu and Tuesdays at Troy Bar, performing with music didn't come naturally to me. And when I received my rounds of applause, they felt undeserved.

'They're clapping for the band, not for you, stupid,' said my inner critic.

Poets like Gil Scott-Heron, Linton Kwesi Johnson and Ursula Rucker could ride a beat skilfully, but not me. I wasn't born to do it. I was doing it to impress Mummy. Maybe music industry success seemed to be within the realm of possibility for me because Little Sis's dad had a number 1 hit in the nineties. But he was not my dad, and his musicality and industry know-how were not passed down to me, not by nature and not by nurture. In my pursuit of a Mummy-approved music career I'd half-convinced myself that music might be how my voice would reach a wider audience, but my songs barely made a splash beyond a few spins on a few national radio stations BBC Radio 1, 1Xtra and BBC Radio 6 Music. It was quite something, it was impressive to some, but it didn't make me happy.

'Do what makes you happy.'

Writing poetry makes me happy. I wanted to write poetry. That was it! Not music. I preferred my spoken word poems stripped back and unaccompanied like I'd seen and heard on *Def Poetry Jam*.

By 2012 I was a member of three poetry collectives – Keats House Poets, Point Blank Poets and Roundhouse Poetry Collective – and some years later I joined Malika's Poetry Kitchen. I can barely begin to explain the confluence of these collectives merging in me, my voice, my personality, my abundance and prosperity. To write that part of my story would ruffle many feathers because it would be impossible to unpick one poet from another in the rich tapestry of my influences.

'He is his biggest influence.'

While what Benjamin Zephaniah once said about me may well be true, I vibe with the South African philosophy 'ubuntu': 'I am because we are.' Poetry has taken me on many work trips abroad, far and wide, from South Africa to North America, the Czech Republic, Germany, India, Ireland, Italy, the Netherlands, Saint Lucia, Sweden and across the UK.

I know I'm lucky. One of my aunts has a singing voice that's similar to Anita Baker's but she hasn't had the kinds of opportunities I've had with poetry to share my voice with the world. I've flown the nest many times over the decades, not just from family homes but also from temporary homes made with actors, dancers, DJs, drag queens, models, musicians, music producers, poets and priests.

The lyrics of my song with Artful were about throwing yourself in at the deep end, and I certainly felt out of my depth in his studio. Poetry was my first love. Writing and recording songs, I feel limited. Whereas writing poems, I feel limitless. Our song was aired on national radio, but thankfully it can't be found online.

Nonetheless, I hope I get many more invitations and opportunities like this that challenge and frighten me. I feel fortunate to have a voice, something to say and many mediums by which to speak up, from spoken word poetry to published poetry collections, from novels in verse to children's picture books, from this memoir to whatever comes next.

Asking For Help

'Yes. Yes please,' I said as I wiped my cheeks and dried my eyes.

I wasn't planning on asking for help, but I was relieved someone had offered it.

I wasn't enjoying the sex I'd been having but I couldn't stop myself. I thought of how Bapou couldn't stop smoking even when he developed a chronic cough.

In my late twenties I gave a doctor or nurse at a sexual health clinic an honest account of the number of sexual partners I'd had in the three months since my last visit. I broke down in tears, shocked to be given the all-clear after a wild couple of months. After they'd handed me a tissue, this person asked if I'd like to be referred to a clinical psychologist.

It was free of charge on the NHS. It was a lifeline. I told the clinical psychologist I was having risky sex and suicidal thoughts. He diagnosed me with depression and anxiety. This was no surprise to me. He offered me medication, but I turned it down. He helped me process some of the trauma of my teens and twenties with talking therapy. It's a process that's ongoing with my new therapist, an integrative arts psychotherapist. I've worked with half a dozen mental health professionals between the first and the latest, and it's still painful for me to revisit certain parts of my past.

Moving back to London after three years living in Glasgow, I realised how much safer I'd felt in Scotland. I felt safer in Scotland because no traumatic incidents happened to me there. No homophobic attacks. No sexual assaults. No muggings. I associated all that with London. I knew those kinds of things happened in Scotland too, but they hadn't happened to me. They hadn't happened to me in Scotland.

My boyfriend, The Doctor, and I talk about the future more than we talk about the past. We talk about a near future where we buy a home together. We talk about a near future where we might live apart if one of us works abroad. We talk about a near future where we take career breaks and pack our lives into The Doctor's white camper van.

We talk about a future where we write a book together. We talk about a future where we write a film or TV script together. We talk about a future where we raise foster children. We talk about a future where we run a small arts space and café together. We talk about a future where we run an artists' and writers' retreat in the Scottish Highlands. The Doctor would cook, maintain the building and be our on-site medic. I'd keep us on schedule, keep the place clean and manage wellbeing.

We've written our wills in conversation with one another. We've talked about the end of life care we would want in various scenarios. We've talked about where he'd like his ashes scattered and where I'd like to be buried. We've discussed important details of our lives up until the moment of our deaths and beyond. But what matters to me is the quality of life we have together. It doesn't matter to me that our bodies will be laid to rest or scattered separately. What matters to me is the quality of love we have while we're together. I know The Doctor feels similarly because we've told each other.

I've felt confident using my voice on stage from a young age, but it's taken a long time for me to learn to speak up for myself in my private life. Since I've started talking therapy, I've felt safer to speak up for myself in private moments without an audience.

HEART

In My Heart of Hearts

Mummy told me it took her ages 'to pluck up the courage to go to an English church'. She thought they'd judge her for being an unmarried mother. Mummy was baptised in the Greek Orthodox Church but sent me and Little Sis to C of E schools. I can understand that since her Cypriot parents had kicked her out of home for having me out of wedlock, she might not have felt it necessary to indoctrinate me into their church.

I wanted there to be continuity between school and home. On my insistence, Mummy took me to the youth club in our local C of E church hall and, thanks to a warm invitation from the mum who ran the youth club, we started to attend the family service on Sunday mornings at 11 a.m., which was followed by biscuits with diluting juice for the children and tea and coffee for adults. Mummy eventually joined the local church choir and helped with Sunday school.

When I asked Mummy about her faith, she said, 'I don't understand it enough to talk about it.' She offered me no religious guidance at home even when asked. But, by her example rather than her words, Mummy showed me that church was important enough to attend the Sunday morning services and volunteer additional time to other activities at church and in the community. We raised money for charities. We visited a local care home to sing Christmas carols annually.

I asked to be baptised and confirmed at fifteen, the same year I came out. Lots of things I was taught in confirmation classes didn't make sense, but I was of the mind that I'd grow in my understanding and faith, and baptism and confirmation were early steps on a long journey.

I believed the path to a Christ-like life would be illuminated at my first communion. As the consecrated host, the body and blood, the sacrifice of Christ, passed through my teenage lips and into my body, I knew deep down in my heart the only way to be with Him would be to remain a virgin, to suppress my sexual appetite for men, to reject part of myself, the part that would surely lead me down a path of sin.

I couldn't reject myself. I chose to reject Him. In the space of a year, I'd turned away from receiving the body and blood of Christ and towards receiving the dicks and semen of older men.

A deeply disturbing trend among the white men was them asking about my ethnicity. Even in my twenties and thirties when I was having sex with white men my age, this line of questioning remained a common one. They would ask me where I was from, I'd tell them 'London', they'd ask where my parents were from. 'London' I'd repeat, and they would ask where my family were from originally. When I told them Mummy's family were Cypriot and my dad's family were Jamaican, nine times out of ten they said something to the tune of, 'So you inherited your big black dick from your Jamaican dad, did you?'

I felt sick to my stomach. I knew I had my dad's face, but this question was beyond the pale. I was naked and vulnerable; my dick size was racialised. Every time this question was asked, or the suggestion was made that my dick size must correlate with my dad's dick, that it must be inherited, must be genetic, that my dick was a Jamaican dick, and I had my Jamaican dad to thank for it, every time I heard this and didn't challenge it, I left feeling more and more objectified. Reduced to the size of my Jamaican erection.

I'm 'versatile' when it comes to anal sex, I'm happy to both 'give' and 'receive'. But when I'm looking for sex online, I say I'm 'bottom', I want to receive. When I'd meet up with men that I'd spoken to online who said they wanted to fuck me, they'd turn around and say they wanted to try and take my dick and ask me to fuck them. I've had men lay me on my back and mount my dick and ride it like a bull rider at a rodeo. I didn't buck like a bull, I'd lie still, and they'd make all the motion for themselves, grinding down onto my dick and moving backwards and forwards with their hips. I was used as a human dildo. Even when they sucked my dick, which I liked, they'd stop midway to say, 'it's so big' and 'it's so thick', and I'd dissociate from 'it', my dick.

Language matters to me in a way that I don't know if it matters to everybody. If someone says, 'it's so big', it seems like it's a separate entity. If someone says, 'your dick is so big', I'm reminded that they are talking about part of my body, part of me. I haven't discovered the root cause of this, but it can be that easy for me to dissociate from or to associate with my body.

Growing up in the church, my idea of right and wrong was linked to the idea of virtue and vice, good and evil, heaven and hell.

As a young child, the idea of God meant I needn't be lonely. God was a great imaginary friend. At least, that's what he seemed to be for Granny. I needed God to be something else for me. God as 'Heavenly Father' meant I had a dad. God was a good dad. Praying to him meant I had someone to talk to. God was a great listener. Church was a welcoming place of prayers and hymns I had memorised. My as-yet-undiagnosed dyslexia didn't trip me up there. Church was a safe space.

I was taught that all sex outside marriage was a sin, not only sex between two men. However, this felt homophobic to me, especially since same-sex marriage wasn't legal when I was growing up.

As a sexually active sixteen-year-old, I didn't want God watching me sucking dicks and getting fucked. I didn't want to repent. Casual sex felt wrong to me, but not because I thought it was a sin. Casual sex felt wrong because I was trying to find my Prince Charming. And yet I was sloshing around in a bucket of frogs. No shade to frogs, or to the people I've had sex with, but it's going to take a lot more talking therapy to change how I feel about this.

I didn't want to jump through theological hoops to explain to myself and others why and how I could be a practising homosexual and a practising Christian. I found corners of Christianity that accepted sexually active queer people. I also searched to find other religions that might've accepted me, namely the Dharmic religions. But ultimately, I decided I didn't need a religion to accept me. I didn't need a god to accept me. What I needed most was to accept myself.

If I were straight, I might still be a Christian. If I could be celibate and happy about it, I might still be a Christian. If I were born today rather than in the eighties, I might grow up to be happily queer and Christian. Queer religious people have existed for as long as there has been religion, but I'm not one of them.

Friends insist I'm a 'spiritual' and 'soulful' person because

I practise yoga and meditation. In my heart I'm neither spiritual nor soulful. The yoga I've practised is a way to connect to my body. Before practising yoga, I dissociated from parts of my body or my body as a whole. My arse or dick in the bedroom. A performance persona or alter ego on stage. Through practising yoga I've come to appreciate my body beyond how it performs in the bedroom or on stage. My body doesn't have to perform well to be worthy. It's enough for my body to simply be. In the moment. In the world.

When I went on a ten-day silent meditation retreat, I wanted to escape from my busy life. I found silence could be golden if it was something you had chosen. The silence of the retreat reminded me of Yiayia and Bapou's garden, a silence that felt safe to me.

I returned to a packed schedule of writing deadlines, meetings, work and social lunches and parties. I'd tell people I'd returned from a silent meditation retreat, and they'd look at me with admiration and say things like, 'Wow! I don't think I could do that.' People's instincts often tell them they're not capable of doing anything outside their norm. When I continued my meditation practice with an app on my mobile phone, I found meditating for ten minutes at home harder than ten days on a silent retreat. It's all about context.

The Greek Orthodox custom of wearing black for forty days helped me process my grief for Bapou, but I had no desire to explore the Greek Orthodox religion any further. The unblinking blue Evil Eye, a symbol of protection, has been a constant in my life, and The Doctor and I have them in our home – in the hallway, bedroom and kitchen – because they remind me of my Cypriot culture and the loving family I come from. That said, I grew up in a house with decorative Buddha statues and no mention of Buddhism. I grew up going to Diwali fireworks displays and Hindu temples at the invitation of our Indian neighbours.

While I don't see myself as a spiritual person, my heart is open to spiritual people, symbols and practices. As a child, I wore a crucifix. In my teens, the pendants I wore were a black and white Yin Yang, an Evil Eye pendant and a gold scroll bearing my name in ancient Egyptian hieroglyphs bought on a trip we took from Cyprus to Egypt to visit the Sphinx and the Giza Pyramids as well as Cairo's archaeological museum. (I told Mummy that when I died, I wanted to be mummified and entombed in a pyramid, but in the meantime, I wanted to sleep in a coffin like a vampire. Mummy said no to me sleeping in a coffin. But she had already said yes to my pet snake Ben, despite the associations with Satan, because I paid for him with my West End money.)

As an adult, I sometimes wear a beaded necklace of jasper that was a gift from Little Sis. I keep a pouch of gemstones by my bedside (aquamarine, citrine, rose quartz and sodalite), and a six-inch-tall ornamental organite pyramid with an ankh (an ancient Egyptian hieroglyphic symbol used to represent 'life') set into it – all gifts from Little Sis.

I've fasted with Muslim friends at university. I've prayed with Christian friends who wanted to pray with me. Granny prays for me at Christmas and on my birthday. I've listened to friends talk about star signs and how heavenly bodies may be affecting us here on Earth. I'm a Scorpio and The Doctor is a Libra. Friends have told us that we're enemy star signs. Apparently, our incompatibility is written in the stars, but I've chosen not to believe this.

I've been friends with self-proclaimed shamans and witches. I've let friends give me tarot card readings and suspended my disbelief because you can't hear people properly unless you listen to them on their own terms. I've wanted to connect with people, heart to heart, meet them where they're at.

I think of when my two nieces want me to play with Barbies and other dolls. I'm not as into dolls as when I was a little boy, but I can see why having a Black Little Mermaid Ariel doll with red dreadlocks means the world to Niece Two. I can pretend we're under the sea when we're splashing this doll's iridescent mermaid tail in the sink. I see religious and spiritual people as being like children who are keen to share their favourite toys with me; it would feel cruel to dismiss them when, as a professional storyteller and a loving uncle, I'm more than capable of playing make-believe.

When people have spoken to me of heavenly powers or earthly energies, I've listened with an open heart and mind. When a close friend told me they thought atheism was a response to religious trauma, my first thought was of my own history with Christianity. I wondered if religious trauma could be the root cause of my atheism. I've engaged in many religious and spiritual practices since I left the church, but in my heart of hearts I still don't believe in God or a higher power. I don't believe in heaven or hell, spirit or soul. I believe when someone dies, they cease to exist.

Heart Attack

Bapou has had a heart attack. We've flown from London to Larnaca, Cyprus. When we arrive, Bapou is in a private room hooked up to drips and machines. He's bare-chested, with a thin white blanket over his pot belly. His hands atop the blanket make his belly look even more pronounced. With a shaky hand, Bapou removes his oxygen mask and says in Greek: 'Thélo na petháno. Den tha me afísoun na petháno.' Meaning: 'I want to die. They won't let me die.'

The hospital staff swoop in to shush him. One of them takes the oxygen mask from Bapou's hand and places it back on his face. They tighten the straps on either side. I feel like Bapou's body is being violated and his feelings are being invalidated. I know the feeling. I think of the times I've been shushed and hands have clasped my mouth. I feel a knot in my stomach.

While a nurse goes on to busy themselves with checking Bapou's vitals, a doctor addresses Mummy and her siblings. They speak in Greek. I've been learning Greek with an app on my mobile phone. What I understand is there's nothing they can do for Bapou besides make him comfortable. He'll die in a matter of days, they say. I've been expecting Bapou's death for decades owing to his chronic cough and refusal to stop smoking. Bapou had ignored his body's distress. When Bapou coughed violently I pictured the bronchial trees in his lungs being felled, making it harder for him to breathe. But it was his body and his choice to make. I accept Bapou is dying, but Mummy and her siblings don't.

Outside the room and in English they discuss whether they're going to get a carer to live with Yiayia and Bapou when he leaves hospital. They agree Yiayia has been doing her best to care for Bapou, but she's going to need help going forward. A nurse, perhaps a cleaner as well. But will Yiayia allow that? they ponder among themselves.

Inside the room Yiayia remains silent in her chair observing the scene. An unmoved queen. This is the last time she will see her husband alive. She knows it as well as I.

I move to the open door and try to interject: Bapou won't be leaving the hospital alive. I'm brushed off like a child rather than a 32-year-old man.

Yiayia doesn't join us on our subsequent hospital visits. We spend a week visiting Bapou every day before he dies one night after visiting hours. The hospital calls the house phone at Yiayia and Bapou's Larnaca house to break the news and give us the opportunity to come and see him one last time before his body is taken to the morgue.

When we arrive Bapou looks like he's sleeping peacefully. His bare chest is still warm when I put my hand to his heart. His forehead is still warm when I kiss it. In doing this, I realise this is the most tender physical moment I've had with Bapou, but he's already gone.

I take a step back and take a photo of Bapou's dead body. This isn't the first photo I've taken of him this week in hospital. I have a close-up photo of the cannula in his right hand. I have a wide shot of Mummy and her siblings, around his bedside.

I took even more photos at Bapou's funeral. By stepping back and documenting this time, I didn't have to be in my body. I didn't have to be in my family. I was an observer. Though I was there, though I took these photos, I still can't recall the smell of incense and chants of the full-bearded Greek Orthodox priest at Bapou's funeral.

The sensory, bodily memory I have of those weeks in Cyprus is of putting my hand to Bapou's chest and kissing the forehead of his still-warm dead body.

As Bapou's coffin is lowered into the ground, a piece of my heart is buried with him, the piece that contained all the pain of losing him. I breathe a sigh of relief that this ordeal is over. I'm awash with relief. Now he's dead, I no longer have to worry about him dying.

I naïvely believe my pain will be buried with Bapou's dead body. I don't know what grief will feel like. How it will come in waves. How I can feel fine one day and be floored by it the next. I don't understand how I can be playing happily with my nappy-clad niece for the whole day after Bapou's funeral, but not have the strength to get out of bed the next.

'Uncle Dean, wake up.' I ignore my niece's tiny knock on my bedroom door in the morning.

When Mummy sends her away and tiptoes in to ask if I want breakfast, I say no. When Mummy comes back later to ask if I want lunch, I say no. When Mummy returns that evening to ask if I want dinner I say 'No' for a third and final time. I am awash with grief.

My grief for Bapou is wrapped up in my upset at my lack of language, at not being a Greek speaker, not getting to know him better, not coming out to him, not letting him know me.

My grief for Bapou is wrapped up in the absence of my dad from my daily life, making Bapou and my uncles crucial role models.

My grief for Bapou is wrapped up with the depression

I've lived with since my teens. I was envious that Bapou got to die while I was still alive. 'Thélo na petháno,' Bapou had said, and he did.

I should be so lucky, I thought.

Grief felt almost identical in my body to depression. Cocooned duvet days, a butterfly too weak to fly. When I'm depressed, I don't feel any appetite for food. Eating feels like one of many pointless activities I must drag myself through so as not to raise alarm bells with my loved ones.

When I'm depressed everything feels pointless: bathing, responding to emails and messages. The almost identical experience of grief – with its tearfulness, tiredness, sleeplessness, loss of appetite for food and sex and loss of interest in everyday activities – has a clear cause one can name, talk about, and is understood and accommodated by so many more people.

My experience of grief for Bapou made me wonder if the depression I'd experienced since my teens was an ambiguous grief for a loss I couldn't name. I thought of how my dad stayed upstairs in his bedroom at Granny's and I wondered if he was depressed. I wondered if I'd inherited depression from my dad as well as his face.

'You had a good sleep yesterday?' Yiayia asks with a laugh, the next day, when I rejoin my family downstairs for breakfast. Yiayia wears a bright floral summer dress, while the rest of the family, including me, are dressed in black. We'd agreed to follow the Greek Orthodox custom of wearing black for forty days as a sign of our mourning for Bapou. A uniform of grief.

Widows like Yiayia would customarily wear black for two years. Unorthodox Yiayia wore black on the day of Bapou's funeral and went back to her floral summer dresses thereafter. This was frowned upon by the rest of the family, but I respected the courage of her conviction if she'd decided that this tradition didn't feel right for her.

Wearing black felt right for me. But because of the Islamophobic comment from my old colleague when I'd had a long, full beard, I decided not to follow the directive for males not to shave for forty days. I kept my beard short and neat in an attempt to keep my grief tidy and discreet.

Back in London, and on the forty-first day Mummy tells me, 'We don't have to wear black any more.' Mummy wears light blue Levi's jeans and a white top. I'd become accustomed to wearing black by then. I had the black trousers, shirt and shoes I'd worn for Bapou's funeral, a pair of black jeans, black t-shirts, black tracksuit bottoms and a black hoodie, a black baseball cap and two black jackets. My mourning suit suited me. My uniform of grief.

I attend an event at an east London private members' club wearing the black baseball cap with a long black jacket over my black jeans and hoodie combo and a friend says, 'Dean, is that you? You look like a low-key celebrity.'

This was a friend I'd once kissed but not a friend I felt comfortable enough with to tell them I wore black to mourn my grandfather. To tell them I'd kissed the forehead of his still-warm dead body. To tell them anything about Bapou or my grief.

My grief looks like a style choice. Disguised at best. Discreet at least. Most people don't know the Greek Orthodox context. Most people don't know my grandfather has died. I don't want to make a show of it.

Open Heart

I met The Doctor on the second of February 2018. I was performing poetry to mark LGBT+ History Month at a central London medical school where The Doctor was studying for a master's degree in infectious diseases and tropical medicine. The building where the event was due to take place had flooded. The event organiser apologised in advance to the other queer poet and me should this affect the turnout for our event. The event organiser assured us that an email had gone out about the change of location to everyone who'd signed up to attend and they had put signs up at the flooded building to let people know where to go for our poetry event.

The Doctor was the first audience member to arrive. Seconds before I'd been telling the other queer poet that I was waiting for a hot doctor to walk through that door because it was my intention to have sex with a doctor that night. He wouldn't be my first doctor, I might add. I'd been clapping my arse cheeks to say 'Thank You, NHS' before it was a thing.

On arrival, The Doctor checked in with the event organiser then made his way directly to the vegan buffet table. The fastidious event organiser had instructed the catering staff to put the vegan and non-vegan food on two separate tables. As a vegan at the time, I took this as a sign that this was who I'd have sex with that night. Wordlessly, with a raised eyebrow and a glance in The Doctor's direction and back to them, I let the other queer poet know I was going to make my move. The other queer poet smiled and nodded in approval. Was the fluttering I felt butterflies in my belly or a baser hunger?

As I approached The Doctor, I had no plan other than to have sex with him. I assumed he was queer given that this was an LGBT+ History Month event. I was attracted to him, his olive skin, his large nose and ears. Something about him felt familiar. As I got closer, and he turned towards me, I was drawn in by hazel eyes that reminded me of the contact lenses I used to wear.

The Doctor felt familiar, like a friend, sibling, cousin or neighbour, like he'd been there the whole time. Meeting The Doctor didn't feel surprising. It felt like a homecoming. I wondered if he might be Greek or Cypriot. I'd wanted a Greek-speaking boyfriend for some time since my weekly Greek classes at the Hellenic Centre in Baker Street hadn't stuck, and I thought I needed a more intimate way to learn the language. I also thought Mummy would be pleased if he were Greek or Cypriot. I was already thinking about introducing him to Mummy. Had I always thought about Mummy's opinion when I met a man?

Although my intentions for The Doctor were sexual in nature, I had an open mind and an open heart. I felt like I could love him in whatever way he wanted to be loved. A platonic friendship if that's what he wanted. Many of my friendships with other queer people had begun with an initial sexual attraction. Instant attraction and some ambiguities weren't new territories to me.

My eyes darted down: no wedding band on the ring finger of his left hand. The previous year at another LGBT+ History Month event I'd been told by one half of an older gay couple who'd been together for decades that the key to a long-lasting relationship was to fall in love with your partner's eyes.

'Are you vegan?' I asked, as I looked into The Doctor's eyes and imagined them decades older with wrinkles around them.

The brown, green and golden swirl of his hazel eyes looked like a galaxy of uncharted planets and stars. I thought of Cypriot Uncle's telescope. The Doctor's naturally long thick eyelashes had the length and thickness false lashes had given me in drag as The Black Flamingo. His caterpillar eyebrows reminded me of *Being Human* and *This Is England* actor, Michael Socha. I knew I could look into The Doctor's eyes for the rest of our lives. In that moment, I thought I could see my whole life in his eyes, past, present and future. It felt inevitable, necessary and overdue.

If I could truly see the future, I would've known The Doctor was so far from vegan that in a matter of months I'd abandon veganism. He'd soon have me scooping bone marrow from roasted veal bones with a lobster pick at St. JOHN restaurant in east London, and not long after I'd be eating lobster and langoustine with him all over Scotland.

'No, I'm not vegan,' said The Doctor in a soft RP English accent, 'but I do like vegetables.' Something about his voice soothed and wooed me. We danced towards his bed from then.

The Doctor said he was glad the event was moved to this building because it was closer to his place. He said he wouldn't have come if it was at the previous location. I took note that he lived locally. I took note that a flood had delivered him to me. It felt biblical and destined to be. That's the Christian conditioning left in me. That's the storyteller in me. The fairy-tale lover in me. The romantic in me.

The Doctor and I chatted politely and nibbled the finger foods as others arrived. The event organiser smiled with relief as the room filled with about fifty or sixty people. From the stage, the organiser welcomed everyone and announced me and the other queer poet.

We performed a set of back-to-back poems passing the microphone back and forth like a baton after each poem. We'd performed together the week before at a central London private members' club for a Burns Night gig and we'd each received a bottle of expensive whisky on top of our fee. Tonight, I was sure my bonus gift would be sex with The Doctor.

I had my poems memorised so I could make eye contact with the audience. The room was full but all I saw was The Doctor. He came over to congratulate me after the performance, he said the group he'd been talking to were going to a nearby LGBTQ+ bar and asked if I'd like to join them.

The Doctor and I followed the group for a few blocks and down some steps to the basement bar, we ordered two glasses of wine, we found a private alcove to stand in with a ledge on which to place our wine glasses and without another word we began to kiss. I felt a whole body 'Yes!'

After several minutes of locked lips and hands wandering with wild abandon, we pulled apart and The Doctor asked, 'What shall we do now?'

'Your place?' I dared.

We left the bar without saying goodbye to the group. We left two full wine glasses on that ledge.

Heavy Heart

'Yiayia is dead,' Mummy says.

I'm on my mobile phone four hundred miles away in Glasgow. I'm about to embark on a UK tour for my second young adult novel, *Only on the Weekends*. I weigh up whether I should offer to cancel this week's launches and head to London to be with Mummy.

My inner critic says, 'You're such a selfish person and a bad son.'

Mummy stays silent.

I ask, 'How did she die?'

'In her sleep.'

This seems more of a hope than something Mummy can know for sure. We can only hope Yiayia's heart stopped in her sleep. We can only hope Yiayia wasn't jolted awake suffocating as her unconscious mind forgot how to breathe only to find her conscious mind didn't know how to breathe either. We can only hope Yiayia didn't suffer in a body shutting down slowly.

The last time I saw Yiayia was in west London two months before. Her thick white hair was brushed up and back and she had a peach-coloured shawl over her shoulders on top of her jacket, jumper and blouse. She wore loose navy blue trousers and slip-on shoes.

We went for a walk in the park that Cypriot Uncle's ground-floor west London flat backs on to. My two nieces, aged six and four, skipped ahead towards the children's playground. Mummy, Cypriot Uncle and I kept a slower pace with Yiayia who used a four-wheeled shopping trolley to steady herself. We were four generations of one family. I could tell our time together was limited.

I told Cypriot Uncle he needed to get Yiayia a proper walker. When he said she was fine with the trolley, I turned to Mummy. I struggled to know how much I was allowed to comment on or interfere with Yiayia's care. While I wasn't in the youngest generation of my family, I was still a child to them.

My nieces called Yiayia 'Big Yiayia' because she was their great-grandmother.

This wasn't the proper way to say it in Greek; it should be 'Proyiayia'. 'Pro' in Greek meaning 'pre, previous, before'.

Mummy called to my far-off nieces to come back because 'Big Yiayia needs to rest'.

We stopped at a park bench and Mummy, Yiayia and Cypriot Uncle sat while me and my nieces stood.

Niece Two smiled to garner praise for coming back. 'Are we still going to the park?' she asked.

Ever the pedant, I couldn't help but correct her. 'We're already in the park, but yes we're still going to the playground, but Big Yiayia is tired and needs to rest for a minute.'

'So, we're going to the park in a minute?' Niece Two asked.

'Yes, in a minute,' I said.

From the park bench Yiayia took in the sights of the park beyond my nieces and me, the lush green trees, a football match and dog walkers.

'What's that animal called?' Yiayia asked.

'A dog,' I said.

'Not a dog,' Yiayia said.

'A bird?' I asked. 'Can you hear them in the trees?'

'Sometimes it's in the trees but it's not a bird,' Yiayia said, 'and sometimes it's on the ground but it's not a dog.'

I looked up at the trees. I looked down at the ground.

'A cat!' Niece One exclaimed, thinking it was a riddle or a guessing game rather than dementia.

'Not a cat,' Yiayia said. 'You see them in the park.'

Mummy and her brother looked at each other and shrugged.

I couldn't see any other animals in the park apart from birds and dogs.

'It has fur and a long tail,' Yiayia said.

'A monkey?' Niece Two asked with a little giggle.

'Not a monkey,' Yiayia tutted. 'You see them in the park.'

I had a thought. 'Yiayia, what would you call it in Greek?'

Yiayia scrunched her face as she thought about this.

The five of us waited.

Mummy and her brother beside Yiayia. Me and my nieces standing facing them.

Dogs barked. Far-off children laughed. Birds chirped in the lush canopy of trees above us.

A squirrel popped out in front of the bench. 'Skíouros!' Yiayia smiled and pointed.

'Squirrel!' I pointed and named it.

'Squirrel!' both nieces repeated.

All six of us laughed.

Mummy asks Little Sis to videocall me from Cypriot Uncle's flat that backs onto that park, once filled with our laughter, so I can see Yiayia's dead body.

'Are you sure you want to see her?' Little Sis checks with me.

'Yes, I'm sure,' I say.

Little Sis flips the camera from her face to Yiayia's. From life to death. I know what lies ahead. Maybe this time I'll hold onto the smell of incense and the chants of the full-bearded Greek Orthodox priest at Yiayia's funeral.

My grief for Yiayia is the guilt that I only saw her twice in the last two months of her life, when she moved back to London from Cyprus to stay with Cypriot Uncle because of her dementia.

My grief for Yiayia is a heavy heart full of regret for not knowing how quickly this disease could kill.

My grief for Yiayia is years of brief phone calls.

'Hi, Yiayia.'

'Hello, agápi mou. You are well?'

'Yes, Yiayia. How are you?'

'I'm fine, agápi mou. You are in Scotland?'

'Yes, Yiayia.'

'You are working?'

'Yes, Yiayia.'

'Good boy. Okay, goodbye.'

'Bye, Yiayia'

Her face framed by a pillow now. A pale, gaunt face with sunken cheeks, her dentures removed for a night's sleep she didn't wake from. My mind leaps back to five years before when Bapou died in hospital, when I'd put my hand to his chest and kissed the forehead of his still-warm dead body. The day after Bapou's funeral, when unorthodox Yiayia went back to her floral summer dresses.

I didn't truly appreciate the warmth and stability Yiayia and Bapou had given me until after their deaths. I didn't have a pure or straightforward relationship with them because Mummy had told me about them kicking her out when she was pregnant with me. I didn't trust that they wouldn't reject me if I came out to them as gay. I didn't give them an opportunity to accept me unconditionally. I didn't give them the benefit of the doubt.

That's it, then, I think. Yiayia and Bapou are gone, along with the opportunity for them to accept me unconditionally.

LEFT HAND

Close-At-Hand

I'm sat in a white camper van by a beach on Vatersay, the southernmost and westernmost inhabited island in the Outer Hebrides of Scotland. It's August 2022. This van belongs to my handsome olive-skinned boyfriend, The Doctor. He's close-at-hand, napping in the back seat. The seat is cream with red piping. The Doctor designed the interior of this van himself. It's tasteful. He has good taste.

With my left hand I lift a cup of Peruvian coffee to my lips. The bag of ground coffee boasts that it was roasted in the pure air of the Hebrides. We bought it from a coffee shop in Oban before taking the five-hour ferry ride to Barra, the first island of our Hebridean tour. From there we've driven across a causeway to the even smaller island of Vatersay to swim at a beach with clear water and golden sand. We've swum, showered at the community centre one-pound-per-two-minutes showers, had lunch, meandered along the coast and returned to the van to warm up.

I resist the urge to google 'UK imports from Peru'. Instead, I sit for a moment in the smallness I feel not knowing what other Peruvian produce I may be consuming.

'Oranges?' I wonder.

The marmalade-loving Peruvian, Paddington Bear, comes to mind. I think of how I passed my Paddington Bear toy down to Little Sis and how he's now been passed down to my nieces. Does that make this toy a family heirloom or does he need to be passed down to a subsequent generation to earn such a lofty title?

The Doctor stirs for a moment and half opens his hazel eyes. I hope to look into his eyes for the rest of our lives. He smiles and then closes them again. He is seven years younger than me. Both our birthdays are in October. In two months, he'll be thirty-one. I'll be thirty-eight.

I look at the ring finger of my left hand and wish for a wedding band. I've dreamed of tying the knot for as long as I can remember. Socially conditioned by the relationships around me, as well as fairy tales in my childhood and romantic comedies in my teens and twenties. The Christian wedding vows, 'in sickness and in health', are among the most beautiful words I've ever heard.

I know love is not limited to marriage. Now I'm in my late thirties with married and unmarried friends, I understand marriage isn't necessary for a great love story. Marriage is only one of many possible relationship milestones.

Last year The Doctor took wedding photos for a pair of our mutual friends. We worked the day as a team with the best man and maid of honour, making sure The Doctor only had to worry about pointing his trusty Nikon DSLR camera (the one that made me feel so seen in Devil's Dyke) at members of the wedding party we placed in front of him. (Once again, we were making memories.) We wrangled friends and family and made sure everyone enjoyed themselves while waiting for their shots so I could tick off every grouping on the list made by the bride and groom.

After the wedding, The Doctor and I sat at his laptop and whittled down photos before he undertook the final edits. The Doctor went to the extent of airbrushing out plug sockets. We looked at this heterosexual couple and all their friends and family who came together to celebrate them and their love as if they were under a microscope. There I was beside the groom in a group of his closest friends. There I was drinking a pint at the reception watching the groom and his grandma playing pool. What day like this will The Doctor and I have if we don't get married? When and why would we gather all our friends and family together?

This month marks a relationship milestone for The Doctor and me. August 2022 marks the end of three years of us living together in Glasgow. When The Doctor's job meant he had to move to a new city, we went from two independent men casually dating in London to a cohabiting couple in Glasgow. I convinced myself, my friends and family that it was not a hasty decision to move four hundred miles away with him because 'I can write anywhere!'

Three years earlier, in my first month living in Scotland in August 2019, I had a reading at the Edinburgh International Book Festival and Jackie Kay brought Carol Ann Duffy to hear me. It was a huge honour that two of Scotland and the UK's most beloved writers took an interest in me, then a newcomer to Scotland and a relatively novice writer compared to Jackie and Carol Ann, the former Makar (or National Poet for Scotland) and the former Poet Laureate of the UK, respectively. I didn't get the impression Carol Ann remembered me being at the poets' reception at Buckingham Palace, which is understandable – she looked pretty busy on the day with Poet Laureate duties.

Jackie and Carol Ann had been in a relationship for fifteen years. Drinking red wine with them after my reading at the festival, it was heartening to see up close and personal how these former lovers were such good friends. It made me wonder if The Doctor and I would be friends if we broke up. I'd like to think so, but I wouldn't know until it happened, which I hope it doesn't.

I haven't kept my exes close-at-hand. Sometimes I see this as regrettable, as pointing to a problem with me and how I treat people as disposable, especially those who might seek to hold me accountable for past misdeeds. At other times I think it's for the best to have let them go. To have no hold over their lives. To occasionally wave at them, as if waving at a royal helicopter – from afar.

Yellow-Stained Fingers

He was hit by his schoolteacher every time he picked up his pen to write with his left hand. Bapou was born in 1934 in a medium-sized town in Cyprus called Aradippou. So frequent was his nonconformity and so ineffectual the corporal punishment inflicted on Little Bapou that the schoolteacher tied his left hand behind his back and forced him to write with his right.

Many decades later, Bapou would tell me this story and end it by saying, 'You are lucky.' But I didn't feel lucky. I felt sad for Bapou, who was now right-handed despite his natural inclination to be left-handed.

What happened to Little Bapou was literal violence, but I could hear in Bapou's voice that he had been hurt beyond being hit. To be told your natural self is inherently wrong, and to be tied up until you conform, this was no minor form of torture.

I wondered what else the world had beaten out of or into Bapou. When I hold my pen in my left hand, I think of Little Bapou and how he wasn't allowed this freedom and I wonder what else he might have done had he not been forced to conform from such a young age.

I remember Bapou as retired, but he was working at the beginning of my childhood. His jobs in London were in factories: Guinness, Heinz and McVitie's. He worked with his hands.

Bapou smoked at least one packet of cigarettes a day. I imagined him taking cigarette breaks alongside Black, brown, white and olive-skinned factory workers prior to his retirement. The middle and index finger of his left hand were stained yellow from holding his cigarette between them. The yellow-stained fingers of his left hand told me of his left-handed nature despite him writing with his right.

I paid close attention to Bapou's body. When I flicked the skin tags on his face and neck, he wouldn't so much as flinch. But when I poked his pot belly, he'd laugh.

When Bapou 'quit' smoking when his chronic cough worsened, he'd buy a packet of cigarettes and keep it at the corner shop and go 'for a walk' several times a day to retrieve and smoke one pre-paid cigarette at a time. Bapou took me to a nearby park and we'd go the long way past the corner shop, the betting shop and the glass-fronted barbershop, even though the park was in the opposite direction.

Bapou said hello to Black, brown, white and olive-skinned neighbours and shop keepers. Bapou would buy me a chocolate bar and I wouldn't tell anyone he was still secretly smoking. Part of me thought Bapou might drop dead at any moment, and it would be my fault for keeping his secret, but another part of me knew it was his body and his choice to make.

Like his route to the park, loving Bapou felt counter-intuitive.

I forged a second-hand impression of Bapou from the hurt handed down to me from Mummy. As loving as Bapou was towards me, he was also that small-minded, hard-hearted, tight-fisted man who'd once rejected Mummy and me. Those judgements of Bapou seemed final until the day he died, when I realised they weren't my judgements to make. Hand-me-down hurt no longer served me. I no longer needed protection from Bapou's potential rejection.

I'd decided I wasn't going to tell Bapou I was gay until I was in a relationship serious enough to put a wedding band on the ring finger of my left hand. My relationship with The Doctor feels serious enough now, with or without a wedding. I can't come out to Bapou now that he's gone but I feel lucky to have found someone who I'd want to introduce to Bapou. Someone I'd have risked Bapou's rejection for, like Mummy once did for my dad and me.

Interlaced Fingers

Working our way up the Western Isles in The Doctor's camper van, The Doctor and I have moved to a new camp-site on the island of Benbecula. It's the first rainy day of our trip and we have stayed in the camper van all morning reading and writing. The Doctor typically reads three books interchangeably: one non-fiction book, one fiction book in English, and another in Italian or Spanish. Thanks to his private school education he can also read ancient Greek and Latin.

From the bottom of one of The Doctor's books I see the fringe of a green and gold leather bookmark from Glyndebourne opera house. It belongs to me. A memento from my childhood as a performer. This bookmark bears a gold-coloured crest with the Latin phrase 'Integer Vitae', which can be translated as 'blameless in life, innocent'. These words can be found in a line by the Roman poet Horace: 'integer vitae scelerisque purus', which can be translated as 'upright of life and free from vice'. I consider the difference between 'blameless', 'innocent' and 'upright'. Of the three, 'upright' is the only one available to me at this stage of life when I can no longer claim to be blameless or innocent.

After a few hours of The Doctor reading and me writing, we decide to brave the rain and walk to a local leisure centre to use the swimming pool and sauna. I think of the gay saunas of my late teens, twenties and early thirties that now seem like a distant memory: the saunas I go to these days are in luxury spas.

In Glasgow, The Doctor and I went to a naked swim and naked yoga class on Sunday evenings. These took place at a Turkish-style luxury spa with decorative tiling, wooden loungers and multicoloured stained-glass lampshades. They were nudist meet-ups. The appeal for The Doctor and me was that it was cheaper to use these facilities on Sunday evenings than it was the rest of the week. Our nudity was a way to access luxury on the cheap. The Doctor was already comfortable with nudity. His friendships involve skinny dipping and naked cycle rides with straight, queer, male and female friends alike.

Our nudity was a small price to pay; in a way it felt like a privilege to be comfortable enough to take part, to be comfortable enough with my own nakedness and the nakedness of my boyfriend in front of other people. Naked adults of all genders, some with tattoos and intimate piercings, some hairy, some shaved, some slim and some fat.

Naked bodies in the 21-metre skylit swimming pool. Naked bodies swinging from the trapeze above the pool, naked bodies in the sauna and steam room. Naked bodies in free-standing baths and hot tubs. Naked bodies in all the positions you can imagine featuring in a yoga class. Naked bodies in the tearoom where we'd help ourselves to tea and biscuits and sit and chat in a circle. This Sunday activity felt like a secular communion to me.

When the stained-glass lampshades cast their multi-coloured light on my naked body I felt nothing less than miraculous – tattoos, scars and all. I found our collective nudity a thing of beauty. A naked body told a different story than a clothed one. Clothed bodies spoke of status and style. Naked bodies bore scars and stretch marks. With or without tattoos and piercings, all of our bodies were marked uniquely with skin tags, moles, hyperpigmentation, or vitiligo like Michael Jackson's.

There were rules that we'd all signed up to and I felt safe. It wasn't a sexual space like the gay saunas I'd frequented in the past. I didn't feel self-conscious. I felt liberated, lounging naked in the lap of luxury, while my naked boyfriend released his grip of the trapeze and made a decadent David Hockney-esque splash in the skylit pool.

When we arrive at the Benbecula leisure centre, we can see into the pool from the lobby, and it's jam-packed with families with floats and inflatables. In the crowded pool of white families, I notice a Black man who's maybe a few years older than me with two pre-teen mixed-race boys and realise these are the first people of colour I've seen since we boarded the ferry at Oban and set off for the Outer Hebrides.

Their Blackness reminds me of mine. How I must have stood out everywhere we've been on this camper van trip. How I'd thought constantly about The Doctor and me standing out as a queer couple when we linked arms or held hands, but I'd not once thought about standing out as a Black man up until this point of seeing another Black man.

The Doctor asks at the reception desk if the pool will get quieter. The receptionist says it will quieten down within the hour as most families have been in for an hour already and don't tend to stay longer than an hour or two.

The Doctor and I head to separate single cubicles to change into trunks then put our clothes and belongings in one locker. This all-gender changing area has maybe a dozen changing cubicles, three small toilet cubicles, a bigger accessible toilet cubicle and one family changing room. This all-gender space seems welcoming to all.

As we enter the poolside, to our left I notice the hoist that would allow a person who could not walk into the pool themselves to be lowered in. To our right I see the sauna and suggest to The Doctor that we sit in there before going into the pool. From the classic wooden sauna with a glass door, The Doctor and I watch the pool become quieter and quieter.

The Black dad and his two boys are the last family left in the pool. He could be their uncle or something else, but I've decided he is their dad. They're playing water polo without any determinable rules, hitting the ball in the air and swimming after it if it's returned out of reach. The way the boys laugh and fling themselves from one side of the pool to the other after the ball is a joy to behold.

As we leave the sauna and enter the pool, we decide to swim lengths in the two lanes furthest from the family but their ball strays into our lanes, again and again. Several times we slow our pace to let the ball be retrieved before we continue but after the fourth time The Doctor lifts the ball out of the pool and tosses it back towards the family.

I look to the lifeguard, who looks to be in his twenties and seems unmoved. I look to The Doctor, who is already swimming on. I look to the Black dad, who wades towards The Doctor's swimming lane and stops. I don't sense a threat of violence, but I can sense this man is taking up space for his sons, for all the times he or they were unwelcomed or unwanted.

The Doctor is swimming back towards the Black dad now and I can see the astonished expression on The Doctor's face that this man is stood bang in the middle of The

Doctor's swimming lane with his hands raised for the ball to be tossed his way by one of his sons. I watch as The Doctor veers into my lane and I'm relieved that he didn't say anything to the Black dad. Not because I think The Doctor can't stand up for himself and not because I think he would've been rude or even that he would've got a bad reaction from the Black dad.

This Black dad in the Outer Hebrides, whether he lived there or was on holiday like us, needed this small victory, to take up some space now that there was some space to take up. Now that all the white families had gone. For a brief while, before The Doctor and I entered the pool, this Black dad and his two sons had it all to themselves.

We interrupted their joy. As a Black man, I knew interrupted joy. As a same-sex couple, The Doctor and I knew interrupted joy. We were vigilant when we held hands, hugged or kissed in public in case of verbal abuse or physical violence. One sideways glance from an onlooker and my flight or fight would kick in without knowing whether I was in danger or projecting past experiences onto the present moment. The Doctor and I were a fearful pair. Much of the fear was generated by me, but The Doctor would never force me to do something I didn't want to. When we were together my fears became his fears too.

The Doctor accompanied me on a work trip to India in 2020. On the way to India, we had a twelve-hour stopover in Dubai and chose not to leave the airport owing to anti-gay laws in the United Arab Emirates. India had only legalised gay sex two years before. When The Doctor worked in West Africa for several months in another country with anti-gay laws, where gay sex had a maximum penalty of lifetime imprisonment, I chose not to visit him despite having enough money for the flights and a flexible schedule.

I was inflexible about protecting my freedom and physical safety.

I'm transported back in time to 2009 when I was twenty-four and holding the hand of The Younger Poet. On the south bank of the River Thames on a part of the path where smooth pavement becomes uneven cobblestones. As the ground beneath our feet became cobbled, I could tell we were in trouble. Not because of the uneven ground but because of the sound of footsteps behind us.

'We don't do that round here,' said the leader of the group of young men who encircled us. 'Why were you two holding hands?' he continued. 'Are you gay?'

I thought of my year at Boy School and the group of boys who encircled me and another boy with long hair and forced us to fight.

'Is it any of your business?' I replied.

Hands shoved me and attempted to pull the hood of my grey Nike hoodie over my eyes. I thought I was about to die but I didn't pray to the Heavenly Father or the river deity Old Father Thames. I was godforsaken and I had to save myself. I had to save us both. I writhed to get free of the hands that held me back, while two of the young men punched and kicked The Younger Poet in the head and back. The body is a weapon. I twisted and tugged my body free of the hands that held me, like I was wrestling with Cuz, I pulled The Younger Poet close to me and through a gap in the group, and we ran for our lives.

These young men hit us for holding hands like Bapou's schoolteacher had hit him for writing with his left hand. We didn't sustain serious physical injuries, but we were psychologically scarred. The Younger Poet and I. Bapou and I.

Mummy and the police LGBT+ community liaison officer warned me and The Younger Poet not to take the attack personally and not to let it get in the way of our relationship. But I did, and it did.

I was The Younger Poet's first boyfriend. The Younger Poet had come out to his parents and his older brother by taking me home for dinner. He'd held my hand under the dining table until he felt ready. Then he placed our interlaced fingers on the tabletop between our plates.

'Dean is my boyfriend,' he said, defiant and proud.

When we were attacked, it felt like I'd let his family down. They'd entrusted me with their newly out queer son and sibling. I couldn't face his parents or his older brother. I believed they'd blame me for what had happened.

I ended my relationship with The Younger Poet soon after the attack because I didn't feel equipped to protect him. I ran from our relationship like I was running for my life. I abandoned him. I was the worst first boyfriend.

The same year, I performed at a queer arts festival in London. I'd written a character monologue called 'Rice & Peas' about domestic violence in a gay relationship. I wanted it to affect people the way Ursula Rucker's spoken word poem 'The Return to Innocence Lost' had affected me.

My narrator talks about the tension at dinner and how he suspects his boyfriend has been cheating because he hasn't hit him or had sex with him all week. It wasn't based on personal experiences of domestic violence but on the experiences of friends. The monologue takes place at a dining table and is interspersed by a poetic refrain containing advice from Granny about how to cook rice and peas. This monologue was also a safe way for me to face my darkest fantasy of being in a relationship with a violent man. The idea of violence fascinated me, though I knew I didn't like it in real life.

I invited my dad to watch me perform this monologue.

I'd not come out to him but assumed word had got back to him via other family members I had come out to. My dad and I only saw each other on three occasions outside Granny's in my teens and twenties: one time when we went to the cinema, another time when he made a day trip to Brighton to visit me at university and on this occasion when he came to watch 'Rice & Peas'.

After my performance my dad told me the piece was well written and performed but proceeded to ask why my character had to be gay. He told me the piece had an important message, but I was limiting my audience by making it a gay relationship. That was it, I'd reached my limit with my dad. It felt like I'd been auditioning for the role of his son for over two decades, but it wasn't a job I wanted any more. It was abundantly clear to me that despite there not being anyone else in the running for the role of his son, it wasn't a part I wanted to play.

Under an alternative name, 'Granny's Kitchen', an edited version of this monologue was published in an anthology of new writing. At twenty-four, I didn't know what a big deal this was. I had no frame of reference for publishing. I knew theatre and spoken word poetry. At the book launch at the Royal Festival Hall, I didn't enjoy the moment. I was thinking about my dad's feedback. I was thinking about that homophobic attack. I wondered if I was limiting myself and my potential audience by focusing on gay characters and issues in my writing.

Through the course of my publishing career, well-meaning older writers have warned me not to limit myself by writing exclusively about race or sexuality because 'once you get put in that box it's hard to get out'.

I was free to hold the pen in my left hand and write about anything. And yet book after book I sit in front of a mirror and write about myself. I hear Bapou tell me, 'You are lucky.' I hear my dad say I'm limiting my audience by writing gay characters.

Again, I hear older writers warning me not to get boxed in. Maybe it's a generational thing: 'don't get boxed in'. But I like this box: Black and queer. There's so much I can do in it. And if I want to branch out, I will.

I remember loading an A4 sheet of paper into Mummy's old typewriter and the empty box spaces of my childhood magazine that I filled with pictures I drew on a separate piece of paper. I remember my primary school petition and my early poem about refusing definition.

While I have the freedom to write about anything, the racism and homophobia I've experienced feels urgent. To not write about it would feel like tacitly consenting to it. My writing centres Black queer joy. Interrupted joy. Limited joy. Limited by 'white-supremacist capitalist patriarchy'.

To be unlimited doesn't mean I have to turn away from my lived experience as a Black queer man.

To be unlimited is an act of honouring my parents, grandparents and ancestors, but it's not bound by their approval or lack thereof. It's an act of service to my community without any expectation of being heralded or thanked. It's not looking for my books in the library or my name in the acknowledgements in other people's books.

To be unlimited is to be in community with writers, readers, Black and queer people who have championed and supported me to be in a position to write more books. It's knowing I've taken every opportunity that felt right and worked my arse off every time. It's knowing that my relationship with The Doctor has given me a stability I didn't have running wild and free in London's gay scene in my twenties. It's feeling free of shame for having shared my body with so many men. It's embracing my flamboyant and flighty nature. It's trusting my instincts. It's doing what makes me happy.

To be unlimited means when I think of Bapou telling me, 'You are lucky', it's not only my left hand that feels free but also my whole body. It's knowing Bapou worked in factories and hoarded his money in order to give his children the stability of home ownership. It's knowing that for a time Mummy skipped meals so that I could eat. It's knowing that my dad did make some brief and impactful appearances in my life.

The last communication I had from my dad was a fourteen-word email in 2016. I didn't reply and I've not heard from him since. While my dad's not dead, I've long grieved our relationship and made peace with it being over and, if not over, ambiguous, unfulfilling and open-ended.

I can't say I feel unlimited all the time. I can only say I feel unlimited at the best of times. At times like this holiday in the Outer Hebrides. The Doctor and I sit side by side on the ferry for the return journey to the mainland. Him to my left, me to his right. This is how we sleep in bed at night and how muscle memory arranges us more often than not.

The Doctor holds my left hand with his right and we look out onto the haar. The foghorn blasting. We can't see far ahead of us, but we trust we'll reach our destination, like when we drift off to sleep together side by side and I trust that, as day follows night, he'll still be there when I wake up in the morning.

Busy Hands

It's October 2022, and the leaves outside have turned from green to yellow. Bare branches have begun to appear on the trees like hands robbed of meaning. From the bay window by the space-saving fold-up desk in our one-bedroom east London flat a building opposite previously obscured by trees now dominates my view. Inside I'm surrounded by evergreen houseplants, our potted portable indoor garden, which moved with us from Glasgow to London, along with our furniture, books, clothes, kitchenware, tea towels from Jersey and Scotland, fridge magnets from Cyprus, Malta and Tenerife.

The cold air teases in draughts and breezes. The bay window is sentinelled by two heavy William Morris curtains, unmoved except by human hands. I can't remember most of September.

The Doctor told me I was shouting in an online meeting last month. He was off work with a cold. He was sat at his laptop where I typically sit by the bay window at the desk. I was at the dining table with my laptop.

My online meeting was about a work trip abroad I'll be going on in January 2023 with a London-based Athens-born poet. We're going to Greece and Cyprus together for research and writing. Towards the end of the hour-long online meeting, The Athenian had said his boyfriend might be joining us for the first few days.

Time folded in on itself.

I flashed back to a work trip abroad, a literary festival five years before. I felt so lonely that I decided to go on a hook-up app and invite men to my hotel room for sex. One after the other, my usual ebb and flow. Four in total. The fourth man raped me.

I flashed forward to the upcoming work trip abroad. I saw myself cheating on The Doctor. Wrecking our relationship. I saw myself being raped again. Thinking I deserved it.

I felt panicked but I believed that I'd stayed calm. I thought I'd asked The Athenian if it would be okay if his boyfriend didn't come because it was a work trip, and I wasn't bringing The Doctor. That's how I thought I'd said it.

The Doctor tells me he listened in with concern as my voice raised and I repeated, 'I felt so lonely. I don't want to feel that way again. I felt so lonely. I don't want to feel that way again.'

The Doctor tells me I was shaking as I closed my laptop after the meeting ended; he tells me I went to bed and didn't get up until the early evening when it was time for dinner. I made dinner, insisting on making avgolemono soup, my favourite dish that Yiayia used to make. We didn't have chicken or lemons in the fridge, two of the main ingredients of this soup along with eggs, rice, carrots, celery, onion, garlic, bay leaves, chicken stock, salt and pepper.

It was only after I went to buy the missing ingredients, came home and made the soup, ate the soup with The Doctor and washed the dishes that my busy hands reached for my mobile phone for the first time that evening to find messages and missed calls from the producer of a podcast on which I was meant to be interviewed hours earlier. I used The Doctor's cold as my excuse for missing the podcast interview. I insinuated that I was making soup for my sick boyfriend.

I made this soup to clear my mind. It felt akin to meditation. I made this soup to focus my mind. I made this soup to soothe my senses. I asked the podcast producer to apologise on my behalf to the hosts of the show and kindly reschedule me for another day.

I didn't understand what had happened.

My body put me to sleep all afternoon and then focused me on making soup that evening to avoid any further flashbacks of the rape. At least this is how I explained it to my new therapist, the integrative arts psychotherapist, at our first session. We pieced together what The Doctor told me with what I remembered of that afternoon and evening and what I remembered from that work trip abroad five years before.

Hold My Hand

When I was raped, my feelings about masturbation changed. I had enjoyed masturbation. I didn't feel any shame about doing it. It was the safest sex I could have in my teens and twenties. Before PrEP became widely available, I was terrified of contracting HIV. And yet I wasn't using condoms. I'd go to a sexual health clinic to get PEP when I had condomless sex with random men whose HIV status I didn't know. I ran towards my fear and away again.

Masturbating over porn, photos, videos and the written word, masturbating in online chatrooms and on phone sex lines calling from the house phone and having to hide the phone bill from Mummy and later using my mobile phone to call these lines, as well as going on hook-up apps to speak to local men and exchange explicit photos when nine times out of ten I had no intention of meeting up . . . masturbating was my favourite hobby, my most effective form of stress relief and my main reward system. I found masturbating comforting. When completing a piece of homework for school and later essays and dissertations for university I rewarded myself with a wank for every few hundred words.

I didn't have any masturbation ritual, I didn't use lube or lotion, I didn't have tissues ready to clean myself up with. I'd wipe the cum off my dick with the inside of my boxer shorts. I'd made the decision to start doing my own laundry to save myself any embarrassment with Mummy. I wasn't addicted to masturbation. I didn't take any unnecessary risks to do it. I didn't do it at school or in public places, but when I was home alone, I found myself masturbating. I didn't often plan it.

Unless I was putting something like a carrot up my arsehole, for which I needed a condom, some lube, tissue and a plastic bag for quick disposal in the outside wheelie bin. This idea didn't come from my vivid imagination or something I'd seen in porn. Someone I'd spoken to online suggested I try it to get my hole ready to be fucked.

I wish I knew self-pleasuring like this didn't have to be a form of preparation for sex with someone else.

I wish I understood you could have sex with yourself.

I wish someone had told me it's possible to make a healthy habit out of it, a romantic ritual of self-loving, perhaps with lube and lotion, perhaps with sex toys, perhaps without porn, focusing on your body and finding solo stimulation through your senses and imagination. Mindful masturbation.

This might mean softening the lighting, burning a candle, incense or essential oils, wearing something that makes you feel sexy, playing music to enhance the mood; it could include food or drink. Or it could be any private time you find and decide to take your time to explore your body without the goal of climax. Notice and observe climax or the absence of it. Without judgement. Give yourself time. Give yourself permission. Give your body undivided attention.

My excessive masturbation when I had a free house and every night before bed wasn't mindful. It was mindless. This was automatic action but it provided some relief and satisfaction. When I started smoking weed it occurred to me that masturbating felt akin to the high of smoking a spliff but the high of a spliff lasted longer. Masturbating made me sleepy like smoking a spliff did. Weed wasn't always freely available to me, so masturbating was my reliable means of getting to sleep at night.

I swore off sex for a year. This was against the advice of the clinical psychologist who told me I'd do better to change my relationship to sex rather than abstain from it. 'Unless you plan to become a monk,' he added, 'but if you plan to have sex again after the year, what do you think is going to happen when you let yourself have sex again?'

I knew what was going to happen, I was going to go wild once the year was up and I was free from my self-imposed celibacy. But I told the clinical psychologist I wanted to try celibacy, perhaps it would suit me. And who knows, maybe I'd decide to become a monk.

I was at the beginning of my yoga practice with the odd class here and there and feeling good about it. I was at the beginning of my meditation practice too and evangelising about it. And with various forms of abstinence, I tried to get to the root of my problems. I began to understand it wasn't food, alcohol, drugs, or even sex. It was shame. The root of which was 'white-supremacist capitalist patriarchy' and how it corrupted everything around me, including my own thinking by feeding my inner critic. I couldn't change a global system by way of talking therapy, abstinence, yoga or meditation, but I could at least seek some inner peace and build some inner strength. I hoped a period of self-reflection and sacrifice would lead me towards an abundant life.

I was giving the impression of pious celibacy much to the amusement of my friends and bemusement of the men who wanted me. I didn't go on apps or websites to arrange hook-ups, but I'd still meet men in clubs. Sometimes they thought I was joking when I let them know on the first, second or third date that I wasn't having sex with them or anyone until I'd completed my year of celibacy.

It wasn't the strictest form of celibacy. I was still caught up in the ebb and flow of my desires. I allowed dancing, hand holding, kissing and fully clothed dry-humping. I wanted to fully abstain, but I didn't believe I was strong-willed enough for that. While most men respected my limits, some pushed them by reaching into my boxer shorts and grabbing my arse or dick and others crossed the line by whipping out my dick and putting it in their mouth. I was clear what my limits were, but some of these men saw them as a challenge to be overcome rather than a place where we could both be safe. And yet I still needed to cum. I wanked through a year of celibacy and the clinical psychologist was right: it didn't change anything besides temporarily freeing me of my anxiety about STIs. An anxiety that returned once I started having sex again.

Let me begin again.

When I was raped, my feelings about masturbation changed. I had flashbacks of The Fourth Man naked on the bed of that hotel room. He is masturbating because he didn't get to finish inside me. I'm frozen in the corner and won't return to the bed to help him finish as requested.

Fight and flight have occurred, and I'm now frozen with disbelief. I'm physically away from him, but the violation continues.

Fight: I bucked like a bronco. Roughly. I pushed him off me. A whole body 'No!'

Flight: I bolted to the corner of the room.

Freeze: I watch in disbelief as he shows no remorse and instead pleads with me to return to the bed and help him finish, to make him cum with my hand or mouth. I was no more than a sex toy to him. I didn't feel like a full person. I was an object. He'd used my body for his own pleasure.

The flashbacks of the rape began when I was in a long-term relationship with The Doctor. We had a fulfilling sex life in which I was safe and at ease with my body and his. Until one morning The Doctor woke with morning glory and came to the breakfast table erect. He unwittingly adjusted the position of his dick inside his briefs with his right hand while spooning muesli into his mouth with his left.

I exploded: 'WHY ARE YOU MASTURBATING OVER BREAKFAST? WHAT'S WRONG WITH YOU?'

I flashed back to that hotel room on that work trip abroad. I was shouting at The Doctor because I didn't shout at The Fourth Man.

The Doctor's dick angered me, like he was doing something terrible to me without my consent.

I don't want to see him masturbating, I thought. I want to have breakfast. Why is he doing this? If he wants to instigate sex, why doesn't he say so? Why doesn't he lean across the table and kiss me? Why won't he tell me if he wants to have sex? I want to have breakfast. I don't want to be raped again.

The Doctor's dick was a threat. Even though it was attached to a person I love and trust, a person who hadn't caused me any physical harm. I had no reason to be afraid of him. But it wasn't him, not in those moments. In those moments, The Fourth Man was superimposed onto him. I felt cornered in that hotel room again. I had to tell The Doctor what the problem was.

The rape cut through space and time. While it happened in a specific place and time, it sent ripples through all versions of me in all places and times. In the time before the rape, it was always on the horizon. From the moment of the rape, it would always be a part of my story.

In the time between the rape and falling in love with The Doctor, my hook-up style was unsentimental; I didn't care about disappointing random men. When I spoke to someone on a hook-up app and arranged to meet, if I arrived at their front door and didn't like the look of him or anything about his energy when he answered the door, I'd turn on my heels and walk away with no explanation or apology.

Being raped made me more risk averse. If someone didn't look like the photo they'd shared online, I'd deem him untrustworthy and I'd walk away. If for some unknown reason my gut feeling was to walk away, I'd listen to my body and walk away. No explanations. No apologies. Gone were the days of having sex with people I wasn't attracted to or carrying on with sex when it didn't feel comfortable. Gone were the days of trimming my pubic hair, shaving my arse or douching before a hook-up. Some were horrified to find shit on their dick after fucking me, but I simply didn't care. On a good day I was numb and on my worst days I contemplated methods of suicide: stepping into traffic or jumping off a bridge, stepping in front of a train or jumping off a balcony.

I channelled the little energy I had left into completing my first novel in verse, *The Black Flamingo*. Know this: writing that book kept me alive. I made a deal with myself: I wouldn't kill myself until I'd finished *The Black Flamingo*. It was the last thing of any value I had left to offer. If my life had any purpose whatsoever, it was to finish writing that book.

Despite writing a poetry collection, several plays, a musical and songs that were played on national radio stations, I didn't feel proud of my old writing. I thought of the older writers who'd warned me my debut poetry collection wasn't ready to be published. They were right. I felt embarrassed by my old writing and my past self. Even though my debut collection received praise from notable people like Benjamin Zephaniah and Joanna Lumley, I felt distant from that book and the bright-eyed butterfly boy who wrote it.

I felt proud of *The Black Flamingo* from the moment I'd started it, and I'd decided that once it was completed, I could die peacefully. It might've been comforting to me to believe that when I died, I'd be with Bapou, but I knew that wouldn't happen. I'd be nowhere. I'd cease to exist. I'd be nothing. That was my only comfort. Nothingness.

I saw no innate value in my life. I was a burden on the few friends who knew I was grieving and depressed. I was masking with everyone else, including the men I had sex with. When I went out, I'd wear a permanent white smile, like the papier-mâché mask I'd made in primary school. I was playing a role like I'd learned to do at stage school. It was easier to engage with people who wanted sex from me; it was exhausting to socialise with people who knew me, but I had the excuse of having a book to finish, which meant I could turn down invites from friends without people becoming suspicious.

The word 'person' is Middle English: from Old French *persone*, from Latin *persona* – 'actor's mask, character in a play', later 'human being'. I was an actor using my smile as a mask to play the character of a functioning human being. My smile is a form of armour that protects me from scrutiny.

When I'd written enough for the day, I'd reward myself with a random hook-up or a wank if I was too tired or sad for sex. This was the track I was on until the day I met The Doctor. The morning after we had sex and awoke naked in his bed, and he told me I had to go because he'd arranged an early morning run with a friend, I thought this was an excuse he'd made up to get rid of me. I thought I wasn't going to see him again. But then he asked for my number, and we started dating and within a month I asked him to be my boyfriend.

My flashbacks and tidal waves of anger came a year and a half later once The Doctor and I were living together. It was a threat when his dick was erect and mine wasn't. Breakfast was the most significant time this happened, and because we ate breakfast together every day, I came to dread weekday mornings.

We enjoyed morning sex on weekends and our sex life wasn't restricted to the bedroom. My confusion and panicked reaction at the breakfast table happened precisely because he didn't make sexual advances towards me. He innocently and nonchalantly had an erection. It wasn't about him. It didn't make sense to be angry at him for having a hard-on. I thought I was comfortable with The Doctor's body. I was used to his morning breath and the updates he gave me on his bowel movements; we both found farting funny, but his morning wood was no laughing matter.

It got worse our first summer of living together, when he'd sleep in a vest top and no underpants. In the morning he'd come to breakfast with his erection on display, no longer bulging his briefs, now flying free, pointing, waving and winking at me.

'LOOK AT ME! PAY ATTENTION TO ME!' yelled my boyfriend's boner.

I was shaking with fear and anger and The Doctor couldn't conceive of why through the fog of my rage. I was afraid, but all he saw was my rage. My accusing finger pointing back at his dick, my voice raised at his member.

'WHY ARE YOU MASTURBATING?' I yelled. A foghorn to let him know to stay away for his own safety as well as mine.

His hand had barely touched his dick. But I was giving him a bollocking for something he wasn't doing. We were both suffering for something no longer happening. The rape had long been over, but the trauma wasn't. I couldn't let this sexual assault and all its associated guilt and shame claim this relationship as another casualty.

I loved this man. I loved his dick, I loved his balls, left and right, I loved his hands and every other part of his body. The way his olive-skinned limbs would coil around my golden-brown body. I loved the birthmark at the base of his spine that I pretend is his off switch and he playfully obliges me by powering down for my amusement. I loved kissing him. I loved sex with him. I loved cuddling him. I loved making meals for him. I loved meals made by him. I loved driving for miles with him. I loved hiking, biking and bouldering. I loved reclining at the cinema where you can order food to your seat and get a free mini chocolate bar with your hot drinks. I loved our life together and it was threatened by something that had happened a year before I'd even met him.

After rehearsing with a close friend who knew the details of the rape, I told The Doctor, 'When I get angry with you for masturbating at breakfast, it's not about you: I'm remembering the man who sexually assaulted me in that hotel room on that work trip abroad. When I got him off me, he kept wanking until he came.'

'Okay,' The Doctor said.

No questions asked. I was sad that he didn't tell me how he felt about the whole situation. It had taken me so much preparation and energy to say those sentences. I decided it was best to put the whole thing to bed with his 'okay'.

While 'okay' wasn't the response I'd hoped for from The Doctor, it wasn't a bad response considering I'd spent months getting angry at him when he came to breakfast with an involuntary erection. My shaming him and his body for something he couldn't help must've taken its toll on him.

My rage can be frightening. The Doctor told me he saw red, orange and yellow flames, licking, lapping, lashing the air around me and flickering in my eyes like hellfire. I felt seen by The Doctor's metaphor because that's how I felt on the inside, like I might spontaneously combust.

My vision wasn't foggy; it was smoke from the hellfire inside me.

I wish The Fourth Man had seen my rage, my portable, personal hellfire, and been afraid and not lain there wanking to completion while I cowered in the corner of that hotel room.

Other than in flashbacks, I've not had to go back to that hotel room, that city or country. What of people whose rapist lives in their community, their family or their home? I'm grateful that I escaped my perpetrator. He's not my boyfriend, he's not a family member, he's not in my neighbourhood.

Flashbacks are memories your body doesn't know are over.

I wish I'd told someone at the hotel.

I wish I'd told someone at the literary festival.

I wish I'd told someone, anyone, sooner.

I wish I didn't blame myself or see it as inevitable that if I had enough sex with random men, I'd be raped by one of them.

How much is 'enough sex'? How much is too much for sympathy? How long does a rape have to last for it to count?

My rape lasted years during which I was in a swamp of self-blame and self-pity. I tried to write about it to make it make sense, but my body didn't need sense, my body needed safety. It's taken me talking about it, with friends, my boyfriend and in therapy, to finally begin to create this safety.

The Fourth Man's first mistake was that he didn't stop at the time of asking if I wanted to stop. In asking this question he put into words what my body must've been screaming at him. I try to see my face through his eyes, a grimace perhaps, not of pain but of sadness and shame, perhaps I looked away or closed my eyes to make him disappear, perhaps my body was tense, my sphincter tightened, or teeth clenched, perhaps I went limp, dead weight, my four limbs, my dick and my neck flopping like a marionette puppet whose strings had been cut.

Whatever it was my body language said, he heard it, he saw it, he couldn't ignore it like so many men had done before him.

He saw my discomfort. My body's distress. He asked, 'Do you want to stop?'

A lifeline. He asked the question, but he was still inside me.

Had he not asked this question, had he ignored my distress, fucked me until he came and left, perhaps he would not be my rapist, perhaps he'd be another drop in the ocean of men who came before him.

When he asked, 'Do you want to stop?' I thought I was rescued. I stopped trying to tread water. I stopped trying to stay afloat. I believed he had already pulled me into a lifeboat. His question reminded me that I had a choice.

'Do you want to stop?' he asked.

'Yes,' I said.

'Just let me finish,' he said.

It wasn't my choice. He was still inside me. He continued fucking me more vigorously to hasten his ejaculation.

My heart sank so fast I thought I might have died. White noise. White everything. Was I marooned in my mind? Or did I leave my body?

I was nowhere. I ceased to exist. I was nothing.

Then I was me again. I thrashed my limbs through the seafoam of white bed sheets, breaking waves, white horses. Waves of him lapped over me, engulfing me, I couldn't breathe. I was out of my depth. My whole body knew I had to get him off me.

Fight: I bucked like a bronco. Roughly. I pushed him off me. A whole body 'No!'

Flight: I bolted towards the window, but there was no way to open it or else I might've jumped.

Freeze: I backed into the corner. A windowpane to my left shoulder, wallpaper to my right. There was a chaise longue to the left of me and a desk to the right. To go forward would mean to run back past the bed, past him, and he was naked and holding his hard dick, his hard dick that had been inside me, and I was naked too, so naked, and I couldn't see my clothes.

I wanted to moonwalk out of that room not taking my eyes off him for a second. Perhaps that's why this incident is seared into my memory.

I couldn't run out into the hallway naked, could I?

No!

It was my hotel room. He had to go.

'You need to leave!' I said.

'Help me finish first,' The Fourth Man replied, without remorse.

As he continued to masturbate in front of me, I was frozen, and this was the worst part of this sexual assault. There was no misunderstanding here. There was no miscommunication here. There was his choice to prioritise his ejaculation. Inside me or in front of me, he was determined to cum. My distress could be diminished, dismissed or, even worse, enjoyed. I was physically away from him, but the violation continued.

This is a rapist. There are many types of rapists. But he is certainly one.

I was appalled that someone could dismiss me like this. I had learned to accept my feelings and bodily signals of discomfort or distress being ignored when I didn't speak up. But to have confirmed I wanted him to stop . . .

I felt betrayed by the sanctity of words.

The men who forced themselves on me during my year of celibacy also appalled me because I'd told them sex wasn't on the cards and they'd wilfully misunderstood what I meant by sex or else decided I didn't mean what I'd said. That I could be coerced or taken by surprise.

I was still unsure what I thought of the men with whom I didn't set boundaries and limits, the older men whom I gave access to my body in my teens, the men who shushed me when I said it hurt and kept fucking me through my whimpering and crying.

I wish I'd said no or 'stop' to those men as well. To deal with this I've had to convince myself that I didn't want them to stop, I've had to convince myself that I enjoy it when it hurts, I've had to convince myself that I enjoyed it when a man put his own desires above mine, I've had to convince myself that my submissive tendencies were some innate desires or part of my personality rather than what I now believe they were: a coping mechanism, a reaction to my sexual pleasure and discomfort being ignored in my teens and early twenties.

I was trying to recover from multiple sexual assaults – variations on a theme of being coerced, taken by surprise or force – before the rape in that hotel room on that work trip. This was the clearest instance of rape I had experienced. The man who masturbated me in the salty Mediterranean Sea wasn't a rapist to me. The man who dropped to his knees and took my dick out of my tracksuit bottoms and put it in his mouth wasn't a rapist to me. The men who shushed me when I said it hurt and kept fucking me through my whimpering and crying weren't rapists to me. They did sexually assault me, but it was different with The Fourth Man.

I felt no gut feeling of fear when I let him into that hotel room, when I let him enter my body. I didn't feel the fear and do it anyway. I didn't see this coming. I wanted to have sex with him, but when I changed my mind and told him so, he didn't listen, he didn't stop.

I've been on a journey of healing and recovery for longer than I've known The Doctor. He's not my knight in shining armour. He's not my Prince Charming. He's not my husband. He's not my enemy star sign. He's not my other half. He doesn't complete me. He's my boyfriend, my best friend, my man. I choose to let him hold my hand.

The Doctor is my person. I'm his. Every day with him I feel chosen.

The Doctor and I choose each other Every Single Day.

BELLY

Umbilical

My belly once held an umbilical anchor to Mummy and psychologically it still does. Mummy points and names my body. Mummy comments on my belly. She points out the bags under my eyes. She points out if my skin is clear or spotty. She comments on the condition of my cuticles. I don't point or comment on the skin tags on Mummy's face and neck, like Bapou used to have, but I wonder if I'll also develop them with age, to complement my pot belly and runner's knee.

I didn't think I'd have a pot belly like Bapou's. I was warned. I used to tease Jamaican Uncle about his and he'd say, 'When you hit thirty, it appears out of nowhere.'

Like the random objects we found together on the banks of the River Thames, and the other random men that flowed in and out of my life, The Mudlark washed up into my life in 2010. As is possible in a diverse city like London, you can meet people who walk the same streets as you with a different worldview. I was searching for something or someone, but it wasn't him.

My eyes scanned The Mudlark: he was white and slim in multicoloured but dull shabby clothes that hung loose. He was in his mid-twenties, as was I. He referred to himself as 'queer' rather than 'gay'. He was vegan and sober. He spoke with anger, disappointment and pity for his past self and all who weren't enlightened to veganism and sobriety.

I couldn't remember where I'd first met The Mudlark, whether it was on an app, at a spoken word poetry event, theatre press night, exhibition opening, film screening or in a club. But I distinctly remember our first date. We met outside the Royal Festival Hall, which I was familiar with as a performer and as a member of the National Poetry Library on its fifth floor, and from having sex in most of the male toilets in the building. But we weren't going into the Royal Festival Hall or any building in the Southbank Centre for that matter.

The Mudlark led me down to the south bank of the River Thames, where he proceeded to search the mud for objects of interest. Stone, metal, bone, broken glass smoothed on one side by the tide to resemble a gemstone. I found this activity ridiculous, as far as a first date was concerned.

'We don't do that round here.'

I remembered The Younger Poet and what had happened a year before a stone's throw away from where I stood. On uneven ground. A cobblestone feeling.

While I kept my eyes peeled for any threat of danger, I focused my attention on not getting mud on my white adidas Stan Smiths. I didn't enjoy the date overall, but there was this one moment when I was drawn in by The Mudlark's passion. He lit up when he found two bare branches that looked like deer antlers and, as he held them atop his head and looked at me, he looked wild and free. That's what I wanted to be.

While my eyes scanned the riverbank, objects washed up on the bank of my memory: a grey Nike hoodie, a blonde Barbie, a tiny pink plastic hairbrush, a light grey Game Boy, a pink Tamagotchi, a bent out of shape paper clip, a

Blue Peter badge, an orange and white Bic razor, a packet of cigarettes, silver-coloured hair beads, a tub of Vaseline, a black and white Yin Yang and an unblinking blue Evil Eye pendant. I handed The Mudlark what I'd found: a smooth white bone and a piece of glass gemstone. I was acting as his unpaid assistant.

I took nothing away for myself besides old and new memories. I left that first date bewildered and bereft with no intention of contacting him again. I was caught by surprise when he called a few days later to ask me on a second date. He took me to an art gallery, and I took him more seriously.

On our third date he took me to a pizza restaurant in Brixton. My eyes scanned the laminated A4 sheet our waiter had placed into my hand. The menu had meat, vegetarian and vegan pizzas. It listed beers and wines before the soft drinks.

'Get whatever you like,' he said pre-empting the question in my mind as to whether it would be rude of me to go for my first instinct of a pepperoni pizza and a glass of red wine.

'It's fine if you want meat,' he reassured me as I looked at him suspiciously, his shiny bald head, his bright blue eyes and even brighter white smile.

'This is a test, isn't it?' I asked.

He laughed.

When my red wine arrived along with his lemonade, I asked him why he didn't drink.

He said he didn't like the person he was when he drank. Drinking was a slippery slope for him which led to drug use and regrettable sex. When my pepperoni pizza arrived along with his cheeseless vegetable pizza, I asked him why he was vegan. He said he didn't want to contribute to the torture and slaughter of animals, and he was worried about the environmental impact of the meat, dairy and fishing industries.

I was indignant in the face of reason.

'One person can't make that much difference,' I said between bites of pepperoni pizza. I ordered another glass of wine because I wanted to kiss him later and I knew I wouldn't have the courage to do it sober. I was unsure if I was attracted to him, but it was our third date and, according to the romantic comedies I'd seen, time to have sex.

I'd had plenty of sex with men with no dating involved but I was attempting to be respectable. I'd already concluded that he and I weren't compatible for a relationship, but I wanted to have sex with him, nonetheless. I thought he was open to the idea because he lived in Brixton and had suggested we meet there for dinner.

When he invited me back to his flat, I wasn't surprised by the tie-dye fabric draped over his bed. I wasn't surprised when he started to kiss me. I wasn't surprised by how quickly we undressed and found our two skinny bodies entwined and writhing in the tie-dye tent of his bed.

I was bemused when his hands didn't make a move for my arse or dick to signal which he was most interested in and let me know whether he was a top or bottom. We kept kissing and our dicks rubbed together as we gripped each other tight with all four of our arms staying above the waist.

When my hands made their move towards his arse, I was surprised that he reached back to hold them by the wrists and said he wanted to kiss and cuddle but nothing more. 'Would that be all right?' he asked earnestly. I appreciated the clarity of his boundaries and limits. I saw myself through his sober eyes. I had been ready to fuck someone I wasn't even sure I was attracted to. He continued, 'If we meet up again, we can do more. Do you think you'd like to meet up again?'

'Yes, of course,' I said. Not a lie, because in saying it I was committing to meeting him again. The Mudlark had offered me a valuable lesson about boundaries and limits, before the rape, before I was ready for it. The next time we met I told him I thought we would be better off as friends. We stayed in touch for some time and when we bumped into each other, we were perfectly pleasant. But I made no effort to forge a friendship with him even when it would have made sense to do so.

From my limited perspective I had enough friends, so The Mudlark became a new myth. Not a deity like Old Father Thames. Maybe he was an angel sent too early. He played his part in the parable of my troubled twenties. With his veganism, sobriety and sexual boundaries, The Mudlark didn't seem real to me given the history of my body. What I was looking for was a boyfriend who felt familiar. A boyfriend to share food with, drink alcohol with, share my body with, and share my life with. I didn't want to change my lifestyle. I didn't want to feel guilty about my choices or who I was.

Hunger

Eating is an emotional thing for me. My guilt about getting chocolate for keeping Bapou's smoking a secret. My sadness about my dad's absence from the dining table at Christmas. How I cried with joy the first time I tried banoffee pie.

I was ten and at the birthday party of a primary school friend.

'What's wrong?' asked the blonde-haired birthday girl.

'It tastes too good,' I spluttered and sobbed, spooning more into my mouth, the overwhelming good feeling from banana and toffee mixing and melting. To this day, I'll eat banoffee sparingly. I don't buy banoffee pie at the super-market, but I'll order it at restaurants as an occasional treat. Tears still well in my eyes at the first spoonful as if I were ten again.

When I turned thirty the examples set by Benjamin Zephaniah and The Mudlark caught up with me and I decided I wanted to be vegan and sober to prove to myself I had some self-control. It wasn't necessarily going to be for ever. It was a pause rather than a reset. It was a chance to gain some perspective. It was a chance to heal, to recon-nect with my body.

I had a hollow empty feeling. I craved obscene amounts of food, especially meat and junk foods like burgers, fried chicken and kebabs. Most junk food would be consumed after a night out drinking alcohol; the two were inextricably linked.

I started with a thirty-day commitment to myself not to eat meat or any animal products and not to drink alcohol or smoke weed. I reached the first month with ease and carried on from there. I remained sober for a year and vegan for two.

When I was both sober and vegan, I thought of The Mudlark when I let people know these things. Friends and family responded positively. Mummy hadn't ever seen the appeal of alcohol and had been vegetarian for a long time already. She quickly adapted to making vegan meals for family dinners and I discovered an abundance of vegan restaurants across London to which I could take my friends and family, as well as the random men I continued to date.

Many friends who were into yoga viewed my decision to go vegan and sober as a detox or cleanse. Maybe it was. My interest and participation in yoga had increased significantly. In my twenties I'd taken the odd class here and there but on turning thirty I threw myself wholeheartedly into a daily yoga practice. My body had more to offer than sex. My body was more than a tool for writing and performing.

At thirty I'd not had a relationship with my body beyond what it could do for money or pleasure. I didn't ask my body what it needed. I fed it food as fuel to keep going. I drank alcohol to quiet my anxiety and because it was freely flowing in the spaces in which I found myself: theatre press nights, exhibition openings, film screenings or in the DJ booths at clubs. Until I turned thirty, I'd not stopped to ask myself about the nutritional value of the food I was eating or whether I wanted to drink alcohol on any given night.

When I visited Cyprus in 2015 my grandparents didn't understand the concept of being vegan. The first few days in Cyprus, Yiayia kept offering me chicken because in Greek the word for meat, 'kréas', means red meat such as lamb, pork and beef. I had to use an equivalent Greek word, 'nistévo', which is a period of religious fasting in the Greek Orthodox Church during which you eat no meat, chicken, fish, eggs or dairy.

'You're fasting?!' exclaimed Yiayia in English. With the aid of this culturally specific language, Yiayia knew what she could and couldn't feed me.

If I could have carried the Greek word 'nistévo' back home to the UK after that holiday I would have. I knew that in Rastafarian culture the word 'ital' meant organically grown vegetarian food, cooked without salt. But I didn't have cause to use this word because I wasn't Rastafarian.

The only experiences of fasting I'd had back home in the UK was giving up chocolate for Lent or fasting with Muslim friends for Ramadan. My vegan fast wasn't religious but perhaps it was spiritual. I was still searching for something in 2015, as I had been in 2010 when I'd met The Mudlark.

To fast from choice felt like a virtue. 'Choice' was the key word. It couldn't be from lack of access to food or a diagnosable eating disorder, to fast virtuously it had to be chosen freely. It was stoic or something? All I knew of Stoicism was dressing plainly and eating simply, but come to think of it maybe I was thinking of minimalism? I was a magpie for shiny self-help titbits. I didn't make a meal of any one philosophy. Far from a buffet table, my knowledge on subjects such as these was an insubstantial meal; my self-help small talk went well with the canapés served at theatre press nights and exhibition openings where I spent many an evening.

I went to hot yoga most mornings and fitted everything else around it. I wouldn't take morning meetings. If an important person with a busy schedule could only do the morning, I'd wait weeks for them to find an afternoon slot rather than give up my morning yoga. I'd made a commitment to myself. My morning hot yoga practice was a fixed point in my otherwise flexible freelance lifestyle. (The fact that hot yoga made me more flexible in my body and sex became more fun is beside the point.)

The word 'freelance' was coined by Sir Walter Scott in his book *Ivanhoe* to describe a medieval mercenary warrior, 'free-lance' indicating that the lance is not sworn to any lord's services. My services were only available in the afternoon and evening. Friends and family knew I practised yoga most mornings but everyone else only knew that I had 'a morning appointment'. I didn't want to be perceived as a yogi. Yoga wasn't my identity or community. I was in community with writers, readers, Black and queer people. I took what suited me from hot yoga and left the rest in that heated studio.

'Sweat it out. Let it go,' I told myself.

Hot yoga was a movement practice for me, not a spiritual one. It was stretching and sweating. I didn't go to yoga to show off or to make friends with anyone but myself. My inner cheerleader, with a voice remarkably similar to my fairy godmother, Joanna Lumley, congratulated me for showing up.

'Wonderful' and 'powerful stuff': repeated words of affirmation throughout the class, as I moved from plank to baby cobra, downward dog to lizard, and as I held myself steady and stood stock-still in a warrior pose.

I made one friend at hot yoga. I got friendly with Shower Buddy in the men's communal showers after class. His commitment to morning classes matched my own. Sometimes we'd place our yoga mats side by side for class. But, from my perspective at least, our more precious time together was in the showers after class when conversation flowed as easily as turning on a tap.

When we first met, Shower Buddy had long blond-brown hair, which he took ages to wash. This reminded me of my weekly hair wash when I had dreadlocks. Shower Buddy's ease with me reminded me of my schoolmate Secret Crush, but my friendship with Shower Buddy put the Plato in platonic.

Shower Buddy and I discussed philosophy, art, mental health and love with an earnestness that evades British banter. We didn't scramble for the humour in serious subjects. There were no 'don't drop the soap' jokes like I'd experienced at Boy School, because there were no jokes at all. Shower Buddy and I both took life and ourselves pretty seriously back then.

My friendship with Shower Buddy continued after I stopped going to hot yoga. He still goes. When The Doctor and I lived in Glasgow, Shower Buddy and I kept in touch, and he came to visit once.

My friendship with Shower Buddy was healing for my inner child, who had felt afraid in high school changing rooms and open-plan showers, both before and after coming out as gay. What had come out in the wash with Shower Buddy was a secure and platonic friendship. My friendship with Shower Buddy is my new best-case scenario, and since meeting him I've felt awash with relief.

There was no sense of comparison as there had been at school. There was no sexual tension as there had been in gay saunas. Since meeting Shower Buddy, communal showers have been less troubling; I can look men in the eyes in changing rooms and open-plan showers and even make casual conversation with them if it feels welcomed.

A decade after meeting The Mudlark, I've started to pay attention to my belly. The way it protrudes after food but how I can still hold it in to appear flat for a photograph if I so wish. I stand in front of the mirror naked and wonder if I have bad posture or need to eat smaller portions or if I need to start doing sit-ups every day.

I don't expect to have six-pack abs. My younger boyfriend, The Doctor, is slim with strong thighs and calves from all the cycling and hiking he does but he doesn't have six-pack abs either. On weekends, we go on all-day walks and bike rides together. He is on his feet all day at work. He easily clocks up his daily step count. Being a writer, at our space-saving fold-up desk all day in our guest-room-office combo, I must take a purposeful afternoon walk to reach my eight thousand steps, downgraded from an over-ambitious ten thousand. I could easily become sedentary, make a nest of our home and let The Doctor deliver sustenance with his weekly food shop and daily affection.

The Doctor and I wish each other 'bon appétit' before we eat. We eat together at home. We split dishes when we eat out to try as much of a menu as possible. If one of us cooks when the other is out, we'll save him a portion. But it doesn't end there: I sometimes come home to find half a peach, half a blood orange or half a banana in the fridge. Not because The Doctor is saving it for himself for later but because he wants to demonstrate that he thought of me when eating this piece of fruit and wishes to share it with me even though I'm not there in the moment. This demonstrative love reminds me of Yiayia handing me a plate of apple slices and orange segments or a cup of tea and a plate of biscuits.

On my right flank I have a tattoo of a puzzle piece. This was my second tattoo. I call it my 'missing piece'. I named my second spoken word poetry EP after this tattoo. This feeling that something is missing. When people ask what this tattoo is for, I have various answers: my dad, God, the biblical missing rib of Adam. Infrequent contact with my dad, losing my religion and searching for romantic love and a fairy-tale ending caused me years of what I now think of as ambiguous grief.

I've thought of having this 'missing piece' tattoo erased with laser tattoo removal, but I want to learn to wear my chosen and accidental markings with pride. Tattoos and scars alike. Something was missing from my life. A hollow empty feeling in my stomach. An appetite for something I couldn't name. Something food, alcohol, drugs, sex or applause couldn't satiate in my teens or twenties. Now we know it was a hunger for connection. I still use food and alcohol to self-soothe when I don't feel connected to others.

I remember needing to go 'for a walk' to the corner shop to get a bar of chocolate after an argument with The Doctor. He thought I was leaving the flat because I was still upset with him. I had to explain to him that despite accepting his apology and him accepting mine, despite us both owning up to the part we played in the argument, I could not move on from the upset.

A cuddle was not enough, kindness was not enough, sex was not an option – although I wanted to be close to The Doctor, I couldn't imagine kissing him while recovering from the upset of our argument. I couldn't release the feelings of stress and anxiety the argument had stirred in my body. I knew how to comfort myself. Chocolate. I needed to eat my feelings. I needed to silence my anxiety. Chocolate made me think of going 'for a walk' to the corner shop with Bapou when he'd buy himself secret cigarettes and buy my silence with chocolate.

As soon as I'd secured a chocolate bar, unwrapped it and broken off the first piece, I felt at peace before it touched my lips. I didn't eat it in secret as I had in the past, I saved a piece for The Doctor.

A peace pact. A way of reconnecting. A secular communion.

I confess to The Doctor when I give in to the temptation of chocolate and junk foods. I tell him when I order fried chicken, which is every time he works a nightshift. Even though The Doctor and I eat healthily together, the salty and greasy fried chicken of my childhood still feels like a treat, and since he's not a fried chicken fan – I'll suck a chicken bone clean of its meat and chew its cartilage like it's my last meal while The Doctor leaves meat on the bone like food has always been and will always be abundant in his life – The Doctor's nightshifts became the perfect storm, the perfect opportunity to order large quantities of fried chicken for dinner.

I feel a painful longing and find it hard to sleep when The Doctor works nights. I add two or three shots of dark rum to the cola I order with my fried chicken meal. Without rum I can't sleep when The Doctor isn't home overnight. Ordering fried chicken with a cola as a mixer for dark rum is a new ritual that I created to cope with my loneliness in place of condomless sex with random men. But now I'm afraid that if I lived alone, I'd do all three regularly: fried chicken, rum and cola, and condomless sex with random men.

As a child, my grandparents were impressed by my appetite for food. I shovelled down the Jamaican curry goat and rice and peas made by Granny. I piled my plate high with the dolmades and keftedes made by Yiayia.

I confess it took me some time to accept Cypriot food. In my early childhood, on my insistence, Yiayia made me frozen pizzas and spaghetti with grated cheese and ketchup, but often instead of Cheddar cheese Yiayia gave me grated halloumi. Eventually my tastes broadened, and I began to willingly eat the same as the adults. Avgolemono soup was my favourite dish that Yiayia used to make. This was closely followed by pourgouri – made with bulgur wheat, vermicelli noodles, onion, tomato, paprika, chicken or vegetable stock, salt, pepper and dried mint. If you didn't recognise pourgouri when you saw it, I'd understand if you mistook its orange-red colour for Mexican rice or maybe even jollof.

At Mummy's I'd eat three Weetabix for breakfast rather than the recommended two. I'd eat peanut butter from the jar with a tablespoon and drink whole pints of milk mixed with pink Nesquik powder. I was praised for my appetite because I was a growing boy.

At high school, my favourite time was the end of term when we'd have a half-day and a group of us boys would go to Pizza Hut for the all-you-can-eat buffet and short, skinny me would keep up, slice-for-slice, with the bigger boys.

True to Jamaican Uncle's warning, my pot belly appeared out of nowhere as I hit thirty. Granny told me that since I'd put on weight, I favoured my uncle more than my dad. I preferred that comparison.

I compared myself to The Doctor during our first two years together. His professional career, his private school education, his nuclear family, his younger, slimmer body and his ability to speak multiple languages. The Doctor loves languages. He speaks Italian, French, Spanish and a little Portuguese. I'm still struggling with Greek. As I've said, the flipside of admiration for your partner is it can create a false sense of rivalry. Comparison being the thief of joy.

We have a photo of us on a beach in Lisbon, Portugal, in June 2018, four months into our relationship. Him in tight blue and yellow Speedos with a flat stomach. Me in black knee-length swimming trunks with a pot belly, my puzzle piece tattoo towards the camera. When my Portuguese friend handed me back my mobile phone and I saw the photo, my first thought was, I should do something about my belly.

In my belly was the most delicious grilled octopus, dozens of deep-fried whitebaits and an obscene number of pastéis de nata. I wondered what The Doctor saw in me. I felt sorry for him that he hadn't met me when I was younger and slimmer. At thirty-three I already felt past my prime. But I had what I wanted: a boyfriend to share food with, drink alcohol with, share my body with, and share my life with.

It might not be correct to say, 'If my man doesn't have a problem with my belly, then neither do I', but at least it's honest. The Doctor's love for me has improved my self-image. When I return to that Portugal photo today, I realise I wasn't holding in my belly, because I wasn't self-conscious in that moment. With my beaming white smile and sparkling eyes, I look every bit the 'leading man' because The Doctor makes me feel like I am. The Doctor has given me this gift over several years, especially when we're on holiday when he's freed from the stresses of his job. When The Doctor takes photos of me or stands side by side with me for a photo, I feel special.

Insatiable

My sex is male. My gender is cisgender man. Meaning: I was assigned male at birth, and I still identify that way today.

I have to suck my belly in to see my dick when I look down these days. As far as I'm aware, all my sexual experiences with trans and non-binary people were in my twenties. I haven't kept in touch with everyone I've had sex with. I have no idea how everyone would identify today. Some I still speak to from time to time have new names and identify as a gender other than the one they were assigned at birth. I found out they were trans or non-binary from announcements they made online.

I recall some who dissociated from their dicks. I could've worried I was doing something wrong when they didn't want me to suck their dick for too long, but I was a good cock sucker. They trusted me enough to say something about not feeling comfortable in their body or with their dick, but I wasn't able to hear it for what it was. They were sexy and that's what mattered most to me. I was attracted to what I could see. I saw facial hair, body hair, tattoos and dicks. I saw sexy men. I was disappointed when they didn't want to fuck me, but I was happy to fuck them, and they said they enjoyed it. I was curious enough to ask them what sexual acts they were comfortable doing with me, but knowing what I know now I might've asked what person they wanted to be with me. But I didn't know what I know now.

When I write about the sex I had in my twenties, it can come across like I didn't know what I was doing, or I didn't like what I was doing. This isn't the full story. Some of the sex I had in my twenties felt fantastic. There was the three-some with the French men with a mirrored ceiling through which I watched them kissing and sucking me with a chore-ography that told me they'd done this dance many times. There was the man who incorporated smoking weed and eating fruit into our sex by rolling his spliff on my rock-hard dick and biting into a shiny red apple then rubbing its exposed mesocarp on my pert nipple. These memories are sectioned off behind a velvet rope in my mind, protected from the rot of shame that seeps into so many of my sexual memories.

Much of my sexual openness was predicated on my excessive consumption of porn in my teens and twenties. There were many things I wasn't interested in and there were other things I was keen to try, so when a sexual activity was suggested, I could give a yes or no response. I knew the menu by heart before I came to the table. My sexual appetite grew insatiable.

By sixteen I thought I'd seen enough porn and stuck enough fingers and objects up my arsehole to know what my comfortable limits would be. But seeing something and doing it are not the same. Porn doesn't prepare you for what sex feels like emotionally or the cumulative effects of certain activities, such as being consensually slapped in the face or spat on or how someone putting their hand over your mouth playfully can normalise someone clasping your mouth when you're asking them to stop.

If I could watch back some of the more unpleasant sexual

encounters I've had, I imagine sobbing for hours and being re-traumatised by it all. I've put much of it out of my mind. If I had it all on tape, I'd likely be able to bring prosecutions against multiple men.

The rape felt uncannily like so many situations I'd been in when I was younger. But with most of those older men I tensed up or went limp like a dead weight and let them continue until they came inside me, when I would rise from the dead to leave their bed. With others they stopped when I started to cry, but I would more often cry when it felt good, not bad, which was most confusing.

Sex is confusing for me. Therefore, verbal communication is sexy. Enthusiastic consent is sexy. They're important to me because I don't trust everyone to pick up on bodily signals of discomfort or distress.

I look out for bodily signs of pleasure and discomfort during sex. I've spent enough time internally screaming inside to know what that looks and feels like, from the grimace in the face and tension in the shoulders to the arching of the back and the clench of the sphincter. I believe I'd pick up on someone else's bodily signals of discomfort or distress, but I don't want it to get to that point. I'm looking for enthusiastic consent from my sexual partners to the point of us stating the obvious.

Yes, I like that.

Yes, I love that.

Yes, I want that.

Yes, I'm ready.

Yes, now.

Yes, deeper, yes, harder.

Yes, yes, *guttural giggle*, yes.

I'd be mortified to be told after the fact that someone didn't enjoy something but had been too polite to say so at the time.

Recently The Doctor and I went to a local pub for the first time in the run-up to Christmas. We got our piping-hot mulled wine in two thin paper cups with Christmas trees printed on them, and with scalding fingertips I politely asked another pair of pub patrons who were taking up a four-seat table if we could sit with them.

I made myself numb to the heat where my fingertips clutched the cups, as the pair emptied the two spare seats of their jackets, scarfs, hats and gloves, placed them across their laps and went back to their conversation.

Once I'd set down our mulled wine and The Doctor and I were settled, I scanned the room for men. My choice not to be sexually promiscuous is to protect us from STIs. In a world free from STIs – and the stigma associated with them – I'd be a slut. Even in this, my most serious and secure romantic relationship, my attraction to other men remains intact and potent with potential. My heart is at home with The Doctor, but my eyes wander, and I still hunger for other men.

I noticed someone I'd not seen behind the busy bar. It was a man I'd had sex with twice before I met The Doctor. Even though I knew he lived in our area, I was shocked to see him here. I felt caught out, like I had to come clean.

'Don't look now,' I blurted out, 'but I've had sex with that barman.' The Doctor turned towards the bar and my whole body felt tense, my toes curled, and my teeth clenched. Through gritted teeth I scolded The Doctor, 'I said "don't look now". Why did you turn around?'

The Doctor said, 'I just heard something about the barman. What did you say?' I couldn't bring myself to repeat what I had said.

'I heard you,' the person beside me whispered conspiratorially. I raised my left index finger to my lips and shushed them in a playful but firm manner. We both laughed it off, but I was mortified.

My inner critic said, 'Why would your boyfriend want to know about who you've had sex with? He's going to think you're such a slut if you point out every person you've had sex with.'

My inner cheerleader said, 'Remember how lovely sex was with that sweet man. Tell The Doctor what you liked about it.'

Not *now*, I thought and said out loud. 'I'll tell you when we leave,' I said to The Doctor.

As we left the pub, I said a quick hello to The Barman, followed by, 'I didn't know you worked here.' The Barman told me he'd started there recently. I briefly introduced him to The Doctor.

Outside the pub, I linked arms with The Doctor and offered my most jovial tone of voice to explain.

'So, I had sex with that barman a couple of times before I met you,' I begin.

'Oh yeah.' The Doctor laughs. 'I thought as much. He was blushing when you said hello.'

A wave of relief washed over me. The Doctor sounded casual and there was a spring in his step.

I mulled it over in my mind. The Barman had told me I was the first man to stay the night with him after sex and, as day follows night, the first man he'd had breakfast with after spending a night together. Whole feature films have been made from lesser storylines, but this wasn't what made The Barman important to my story. It was the sex itself that was important to me.

Fuck it, I thought.

It was safe to tell The Doctor about sex with The Barman.

'He was really enthusiastic during sex. He used to say things like, "Your dick is so beautiful!", "Your arse is so gorgeous!", "I can't believe I'm fucking you!" and "This is so amazing!" I found it adorable and reassuring how vocal he was. I knew what he was thinking. He said it was because he has ADHD, and he can't help saying what's on his mind. He's the only person I've had sex with who's told me they have ADHD, so I have a sample size of one. I can't form any theories about neurodiversity and communicativeness during sex, but I took him at his word because he knows his experience best.'

My mini monologue lingered in the frosty December air.

'Oh yeah,' The Doctor said flatly. No laughter. Which part of what I'd said was this 'oh yeah' supposed to be a response to?

I didn't say the final thing I wanted to say: 'I'd like it if you could be even more vocal with me during sex.'

I felt a fool. I felt the full chill of the night. The mulled wine in my belly and my bright blue puffer jacket weren't enough to keep me warm. Blood rose to the surface of my skin. Was I blushing from embarrassment, frustration or shame?

My exes weren't off limits. I'd told The Doctor about The Younger Poet and others. The Doctor had to know about my past relationships to understand what I wanted and didn't want with him.

The Doctor and I didn't speak much about fuck buddies and one-off hook-ups because I still felt some shame about that. I didn't want my boyfriend to think of me as a slut, even though the word 'slut' was in flux for me and part of me wanted to wear it proudly like a crown of flowers, one flower for each person I'd had sex with. Now, that would be a beautiful thing.

Free love of the sixties and seventies, before HIV, was being reclaimed by men who have sex with men thanks to PEP, PrEP and U=U. I've sex without fear with men whose

HIV viral load was undetectable and therefore untransmittable. U=U. Nonetheless, the global HIV/AIDS epidemic, which began in the eighties, and homophobic legislation like Section 28 – a law enacted in 1988 in the UK – had a huge impact on me, and I felt the aftershocks daily.

Section 28 prohibited the 'promotion of homosexuality' by local authorities, which was open to interpretation, but in practice meant that school libraries didn't stock LGBTQ+ books, many LGBTQ+ schoolteachers didn't come out to their colleagues or students, and LGBTQ+ students weren't affirmed and supported in the way they can be today. Section 28 was enshrined in English law the whole time I was at school from 1988 to 2003. But I knew The Doctor knew all this, so we walked the rest of the way home in silence.

Gut Feeling

The Doctor likes spontaneous affection. He comes up behind me and starts to kiss me when I'm washing the dishes after dinner. Washing the dishes is my precious time to focus on nothing but the task at hand; I like to zone out the rest of the world and complete this task to the best of my ability. Clean dishes, clean surfaces and a swept floor give me a sense of accomplishment. Sometimes I think I'd like to be a househusband, a homemaker. After cleaning up the kitchen I go into the sala and plump the sofa cushions so I can see it looking show-home-pristine, as if getting it ready for *MTV Cribs*.

When The Doctor, my not-husband, interrupts my cleaning ritual with spontaneous affection I find it hard to respond. 'He wants sex,' says my inner critic, jumping to conclusions that romantic kisses must lead us to the bedroom. But I know The Doctor wants affection and not necessarily sex.

I don't know if it's bad luck or my confirmation bias, but The Doctor often tries to kiss me when I've lifted a sharp knife from the kitchen sink and started to wipe its blade with the soapy sponge. My kneejerk response is to scold him, 'Why are you creeping up on me when I'm holding a knife?'

I was afraid of hurting The Doctor. As a child, I believed

that as the Little Man of the house, I'd have to stab someone to defend Mummy and Little Sis if someone broke in while they were sleeping. In my teens, I was mugged by three boys on my way home from Notting Hill Carnival. I'd been at Carnival with my Jamaican family. The day had been a relative success. I'd been restrained in my dancing. To appear straight, I was mindful of the natural spring of my step and sway of my hips. I kept my true nature captive like my pet snake Ben.

As I left Carnival and bounced back home without the safety of my Jamaican family around, I became a target. One of the boys said he had a knife in his pocket, which was enough to make me comply. They demanded my money and mobile phone but when they saw my phone they laughed and called it a 'brick' and said I could keep it.

Despite the mugging not happening at Carnival itself, I've mostly kept away from this annual celebration of Caribbean culture. I say 'mostly' because I have been to Carnival a few times since, not with my family but with friends. I didn't enjoy it. I saw danger everywhere in a way I didn't see when I was with my family. I couldn't imagine my aunts, uncles or cousins letting anything bad happen to me. But I wasn't sure whether friends would come to my aid or scatter or even notice in a timely manner if I were to be mugged or manhandled in the crowd. Even though I don't go to Carnival any more, I feel tense on Carnival weekends when I'm in London for them.

A knife is a tool, an extension of the human body. The knife isn't what frightens me: what frightens me is our ability to hurt one another. Figures from the Office for National Statistics showed 282 homicides were committed in the UK with a knife or sharp instrument in the twelve months to March 2022. According to the ONS, this was a nineteen per cent rise compared with the previous year and the highest annual total since records began in 1946. I think of Stephen Lawrence in 1993, Damilola Taylor in 2000, Ben Kinsella and Jimmy Mizen in 2008 and hundreds of others killed in the UK with a knife or sharp instrument whose names I don't know and families I haven't met.

I think of Bapou telling me, 'You are lucky!' Is it sad that I feel lucky when the worst things I can imagine don't happen to me? When I'm not raped, mugged, bullied, beaten up or killed, I feel lucky.

I was afraid of hurting myself. I've cut myself once with a knife: an avocado deseeding accident. Only after I'd eaten my avocado toast, did I go to A & E to have my right hand glued back together. I couldn't practise yoga for months until it healed under the glue because if I were to apply pressure to it in a downward dog or a plank the glued wound would split open again.

I've asked The Doctor if sex in the kitchen is important to him. He's told me plainly that it's not about the location, it's about spontaneity. I've told The Doctor kindly that if he wants to be spontaneously affectionate with me, he mustn't do it when I have a knife in my hand or when I'm holding anything else that could be used as a weapon, such as a boiling kettle or an iron, not when I'm brushing my teeth or when my laptop is balanced on my lap. Before any sexual contact, he should at least ask me to stop what I'm doing and put down what I'm holding.

Before we'd had this conversation, I'd tried to please The Doctor against my better judgement by spontaneously kissing him when he was texting. Startled by my kiss, The Doctor dropped his mobile phone and the screen smashed. He wanted me to apologise, but I refused. 'I did what you wanted,' I said, 'and this is what spontaneity gets you.'

I did apologise eventually. I told The Doctor that my fear of spontaneity is a fear that something else will break, something that can't be fixed or replaced. Something like trust, something like self-worth, something like that.

My fear of spontaneity is a gut feeling. My fear of spontaneity is the fear of being raped again.

ROOTS

Root Out

I awoke with a hangover from cocktails and shots the night before. A notification on my mobile phone reminded me that it would've been Yiayia's birthday today: 21 January 2023. I placed my phone face down and the unblinking blue Evil Eye on the back of my phone case stared up at me. I'd typically call Yiayia on her birthday, even though the call would be brief.

It meant a lot to Yiayia to speak on birthdays, Christmas and Greek Orthodox Easter when we couldn't be together. If I was in London, I'd have gone with Mummy to Yiayia's grave. But I wasn't in London, I was in Athens.

I peeled myself out of bed, popped a capsule in the Nespresso machine and an espresso cup under the nozzle, hit the 'on' button and, as my coffee sputtered out, I opened the door to my hotel room balcony with its view of the Acropolis.

I'd die if I jumped from this balcony, I thought.

If I was about to die, I'd call The Doctor, my emergency contact. My boyfriend, my best friend, my man.

'Agápi mou,' I thought I heard. 'My love.'

I backed away from the edge of the balcony. I went back inside to fetch my espresso, and with a view of the Acropolis I set out to write what I remembered of last night, as if it were a pixelated dream I might forget.

There were five of us in total, all queer poets. My excessive drinking was due to my anxiety at meeting new people in a country I'd only been to once before as a tourist. The Athenian had got in touch with one of the poets who'd invited us to meet them at a bar that gave free shots on arrival.

Even though the queer Greek poets spoke English with me, when I left and returned to our table from the toilet or buying a round of drinks the conversation would be flowing freely in Greek in a way that it didn't when they spoke in English. I felt ashamed not to have enough confidence to put together a sentence in Greek. No one around the table made me feel left out, quite the opposite, but I felt ashamed that they were doing all the work to include me.

My inner critic said, 'They'd rather you weren't here so they could speak freely in Greek and not translate themselves for you.'

In English, I asked each of the three new people around the table to tell me about their poetry and their experiences as queer poets in Greece. They were all in the process of editing poems for an anthology of queer Greek poetry. The Athenian would also have a poem in this anthology, but unlike the others he had written his poem in English and had it translated into Greek.

While he still travels back to Athens, The Athenian has lived in the UK for twenty-four years since he left Athens to attend university at eighteen, he has a British passport, and he writes poetry in English. Despite knowing all of this about him I still can't help but think of The Athenian as an Athenian, perhaps because so many of his poems are about Greece and Athens. The Athenian writes powerfully about the Athens of his youth, in which he felt unable to be Openly Queer.

As someone born and raised in London, I've taken my city for granted. I've taken for granted London's diversity and the freedom this gave me to come out at fifteen and find spaces to express myself as a Black queer man and share my poetry.

The Athenian had to move to London to find the freedom I took for granted. Twenty-four years later, The Athenian has found a queer poetry community in Greece that he didn't have in his teens. As I pondered this, I felt lucky to have grown up in London.

One of the poets told me he'd been struggling with a metaphor in his poem for the anthology. It was set at a protest alongside a communist comrade he had a same-sex desire for. He wanted to write of his unfulfilled desire for this male comrade as the unfulfilled potential of communism in Greece. He said he was struggling with an image of tear gas thrown by the police at the protesters – his tears fell not just because of the tear gas but from the frustration of unrequited love.

I suggested he didn't spell out the sexual or romantic elements but let that queer longing exist in the subtext. I suggested he focus on the sensory, bodily memory of protest, standing shoulder to shoulder with his comrade, and let the reader root out the desire for themselves. I'm sure it was the alcohol that emboldened me to give advice about a poem I'd not read, written in a language I barely understood, about a political movement I knew little about, but, luckily, my advice was graciously received. We went on to discuss consent and sexual assault in the LGBTQ+ community.

Because of the alcohol, I can't say if I was responsible for veering our conversation to this topic. Two of the poets around the table were over a decade younger than me. I told them they were lucky to have come of age in a time when they had the language and knowledge to name when a sexual assault had happened to them. I said that even if language and knowledge can't necessarily stop a sexual assault from happening, they can help people process the experience and seek support faster.

Today The Athenian and I go to a bookshop, and I buy a poster I'd seen through the window on our first evening here: a black-and-white print by an artist called Anna Kiosse of an Ancient Greek-style vase with the words 'TOGETHER FOREVER' emblazoned across its body. I love how these words rhyme and chime with my wish for The Doctor and me. Above these words are a black hand and a white hand with interlaced fingers. I plan to give this poster to The Doctor as a Valentine's Day gift next month. It will be our fifth Valentine's Day together. I've been with The Doctor since before Niece Two was born; she has only ever known me with him. This is my favourite version of me so far. The Doctor doesn't typically do favourites; he claims not to have a favourite dish, favourite film or favourite song, but he tells me I'm his favourite person.

The Doctor came along at a time when I wasn't looking for any more than a one-night stand. But once we'd had sex, I felt more for The Doctor than I had for anyone I'd had sex with. It wasn't the sex as such. It was an acceptance of each other, who we were in that moment. There was trust, respect, tenderness and an awareness and enthusiasm about each other's pleasure. Maybe some people manage this every time they have casual sex, but it was only the second time for me, the first being The Barman, and it was a clear sign The Doctor was someone I wanted to get to know. Without The Barman, I might not have recognised the similarly amazing qualities of The Doctor. The more I've got to know The Doctor, the more I have come to understand that his sexual generosity is but one facet of his overall goodness. I don't believe in innate goodness, but I recognise when someone is trying their best. That's the man I've chosen to love.

All these men are connected: The Doctor, The Barman, The Younger Poet, The Comedian, The Mudlark, and even The Fourth Man. Most have never met each other or been in the same room but they're all connected through me, the former paper clip collector who makes meaning from previously unconnected things: stories, memories and men.

Strongest Roots

I take a long shower that included cutting my fingernails and toenails and trimming my cuticles. Pruning and preening. I detach my mobile phone from its charger. I don't attend to notifications. I'm detached from the UK. Not communicating with friends. Not responding to emails other than about this research and writing trip. I'm seeing family in Larnaca on Friday.

The Athenian and I have done plenty since we got to Nicosia, but it's felt different to my real life and my idea of Cyprus, partly because I haven't seen my family and I'm not here with Mummy. But mostly because I'm inland in Nicosia and yet to see the Mediterranean Sea.

The balcony of my Nicosia hotel room looks onto a residential area. A couple of floors up.

I'd survive the fall, I thought.

On one side a lemon tree, two orange trees and someone hanging laundry out to dry. I look up to the clear blue sky.

I remember Cypriot Uncle's telescope and how at night we looked up at the moon, planets and stars, heavenly bodies I knew were there beyond daytime blue. When I look back down, I see Yiayia wearing a bright floral summer dress hanging laundry out to dry and Bapou tending to an orange tree in their Larnaca garden. I see Yiayia cutting Bapou's straight hair. I see Yiayia handing me a cup of tea and a plate of biscuits. I see Yiayia handing me a plate of apple slices and orange segments.

These wordless memories act as a counterbalance to the spoken word poetry that's come to define me. Ironic that one of my early poems was about refusing definition. I still perform often but I make sure I schedule plenty of time to be quiet, to be silent. The chosen silence I learned through meditation, not the involuntary silence I learned through stigma, fear and shame.

I'm glad for this quiet time to myself today. I'm exhausted from the spoken word poetry event we performed at here, in Nicosia, last night. Most of the performances were in English, but the handful of poets who read in Greek apologised directly to me before they began their reading. This courtesy on their part felt humiliating to me. I felt singled out as the person who didn't speak Greek. I felt ashamed.

My inner critic said, 'Your connection is limited by your lack of language.'

It's a pleasant nineteen degrees Celsius today. My leg is shaking up and down. I'm a restless puppy that needs to be taken for a walk. I look for the nearest coffee shop, which is two minutes' walk from the hotel. I look further afield and find another twenty minutes away. I note from the Maps app that my chosen coffee shop is close to a university. There'll surely be people writing there.

After walking along the palm tree-lined boulevard, I discover that I'm correct in my assumption that this coffee shop would be full of young people with laptops and notebooks. Those who don't have their heads in a laptop or notebook are rolling and smoking cigarettes, playing Tavli – Greek backgammon – and talking loudly, competing with a Calvin Harris and Dua Lipa song blasting through the speakers. My quiet mind becomes as loud as the music around me.

I think of playing Tavli with Bapou. I think of Bapou when I play this board game with The Doctor. I imagine Bapou and The Doctor playing Tavli together. My two most beloved men meet in my vivid imagination: a bridge between the living and the dead. When had I played Tavli with Bapou? When and where? In London or Larnaca? It didn't matter. The location was not the point of this memory. What I needed was to feel Bapou's eyes on me as I decided my next move.

I order my chicken Caesar salad and iced latte and take a seat in the sunny conservatory smoking area of the café. I am far enough from any smokers. I move the ashtray to the other side of my table and unpack my notebook and pen, writing between mouthfuls of salad and sips of coffee. From a jovial table behind me I hear the word 'malaka' in every sentence, an affectionate term friends use to refer to each other. It means 'mate' and 'friend'. It also means 'arsehole' and 'wanker'.

'One Kiss' gives way to Justin Timberlake's 'Can't Stop the Feeling!' which gives way to Mark Ronson's 'Nothing Breaks Like A Heart' featuring Miley Cyrus. Slamming of Tavli pieces on the board. The word 'malaka' punching through the rest of the Greek chatter, I zone out more easily than this distinctive word. I think of the homophobic music and comments I'd heard in the glass-fronted barbershop full of Black men referring to gay and effeminate men as 'batty men' when I was a little boy: Jamaican dancehall music and the words 'batty man' on repeat.

When the Black, queer Belgian singer Stromae blasts over the coffee shop speakers I think of The Doctor. We're both fans of Stromae. Despite the overlaps in our taste in music – Beyoncé, Cleo Sol, Frank Ocean, Joni Mitchell, Snoh Aalegra and Stromae – I'm concerned our connection is invisible, ephemeral, like music streaming, like the songs that have played in this coffee shop, a few minutes each before giving way to the next.

A band The Doctor and I discovered together are an Irish folk music duo called Ye Vagabonds. We've been to see them perform four times, twice when we were in Glasgow and twice since we've been back in London. Going to their gigs is a new tradition The Doctor and I have made together.

While we have our shared traditions, apart from a shared tenancy agreement and bills for our one-bedroom east London flat, The Doctor and I have no attachments besides our love and intention to stay 'TOGETHER FOREVER'. Even though our right to marry as a same-sex couple has been hard fought for, The Doctor isn't sure if he wants to get married.

Last Christmas I bought The Doctor a rose gold necklace that came in a little square box. When I presented it to him wrapped in Christmas paper with a bow on top, his face dropped. I had to clarify, 'Don't worry! It's not an engagement ring.'

When The Doctor and I had been together for a year and a half, he got a job in Scotland that would last three years, so we decided that I'd move with him to Glasgow rather than having a long-distance relationship between London and Glasgow. I'd tried long-distance in the past with men in Manchester, which was much closer, easier and cheaper to travel to than Glasgow. These previous relationships had been too taxing, I'd either cheated on or broken up with these men.

I didn't want to cheat on The Doctor, nor did I want an open relationship. But without the physical touch of The Doctor, I knew I'd want to have sex with other people. The Doctor said he'd be okay with an open relationship if we stayed on PrEP and tested for STIs. He talked practically.

I talked emotionally. I was explaining my reasons for wanting to move with him to Glasgow rather than having a long-distance relationship when The Doctor interrupted me.

'I'm not looking to make a home in Glasgow,' he said.

He took the wind out of my sails. A gut punch. I was stunned into silence.

'Game Over,' said my inner critic. 'He's breaking up with you.'

My inner cheerleader had nothing to offer.

My body felt ice-cold. My heart was a stone. I was numb. Like when I heard homophobic comments. Like when Bapou died.

'What did I say that was so wrong?' The Doctor addressed my silent despair with defensiveness. 'It's hardly going to be a home if we're only there for three years.'

Mummy's house had been my home. There was nothing wrong with what The Doctor had said.

My inner critic said, 'Why did you think this relationship was serious? You're an idiot! You'll never know home if you think it relies on someone else providing it. You were homeless for the first year of your life. You could be made homeless again at any time. Yiayia and Bapou's London house is gone. Mummy's house is no longer your home. These London flat shares aren't home. You can't rely on The Doctor to give you a home.'

When I reflect on these thoughts now, they're less painful than they once were. Perhaps this was constructive criticism. Perhaps my inner critic wasn't a villain or quite so wicked after all.

I separated 'house' from 'home' when I moved from Mummy's. I separated house from home when Yiayia and Bapou left London and returned to Larnaca. A house is a building. Home is a feeling, perhaps a choice.

Our two-bedroom, red sandstone tenement flat in Glasgow became home for the three years we lived there. Once we'd spent several weeks decorating it together, painted feature walls, hung William Morris curtains and collected second-hand wooden furniture from houses and warehouses across Glasgow, once we'd filled drawers and wardrobes with our clothes and bags of dried lavender, we began to feel cosy. Comfortable. Half a dozen houseplants and so many rainbows: rainbow coasters, rainbow tea pot, rainbow mugs and rainbow butter dish. My nieces are convinced my favourite colour is rainbow. The sofa was big and comfy and reminded me of those in 'the mermaid room' in Mariah Carey's Tribeca penthouse apartment on *MTV Cribs*. We started referring to it as home and reflected on and laughed about The Doctor's initial rejection of the notion of making a home together.

I've still not let go of my sadness that we weren't on the same page to start with. But once we'd painted those feature walls, hung those curtains, bought new lamps and various knick-knacks for the place, once we'd got to know our local area, shops, coffee shops, restaurants, bars, the library, the bus and train times, it became our home.

My stone heart softened. My body eased into the feeling of being at home in Glasgow. It would confuse Mummy when she called me when I was in Glasgow city centre heading back to the flat in the Southside: she'd ask me what I was up to, and I'd say I was 'on my way home'.

'Are you in London?!' Mummy would shriek with joy.

'No, I mean my home in Glasgow,' I would say, a tinge of embarrassment and a hint of annoyance.

I didn't see making a home with The Doctor as betraying Mummy. She was the one who told me to 'do what makes you happy'. Making a home with The Doctor makes me happy. It felt inevitable, necessary and overdue.

An overdue part of our move was moving my personal library from Mummy's in London to our flat in Glasgow. There was space for all my books, but I waited over a year to move them because I had sixteen boxes and The Doctor's statement – 'I'm not looking to make a home in Glasgow' – had spooked me.

When I moved to Glasgow I took two suitcases of clothes, my in-progress notebooks, my laptop and tablet and not much more. I left everything else at Mummy's, including my personal library. Keeping my books at Mummy's anchored me to her.

I travelled light to Glasgow with two suitcases because I wanted to know I could up and leave at any time. I told The Doctor as much, and he confessed that he found this strangely reassuring. He was uncomfortable with the idea that I'd move over four hundred miles to a new city away from my family, friends and reliable work in schools to be with him. He said he didn't feel worthy of someone making such a sacrifice to be with him. He said it was a lot of pressure on the relationship, on him. This conversation was a breakthrough. I said I could leave if I wanted to, in a heartbeat. We were honest with one another, and we haven't stopped since. This 'I don't need you, I choose you' type of honesty could be too harsh for some people to handle, but in many ways, it has been the making of us. The Doctor has been clear the past five years that marriage isn't on the cards. While I've accepted this, when I'm feeling anxious it can feel like a puzzle, a problem to be solved. How do we fit into each other's lives?

When we combined our personal libraries a year into living together in Glasgow, our differences were made manifest through them. His books are mostly medical, nature writing and other non-fiction, while my books are mostly poetry, self-help and young adult fiction. Our only duplicates are *On Earth We're Briefly Gorgeous* by Ocean Vuong and *The Master's Tools Will Never Dismantle the Master's House* by Audre Lorde. Our overlap with books is so slight, but I tell myself this means we have that much more to offer each other.

In a few days I'll go to Larnaca to visit my great-aunt and great-uncle, whom I call Theía and Theío. Two of the strongest roots of my Cypriot family tree. I've not come out to them.

My Cypriot and Jamaican family all know they have a writer in their midst, but beyond Mummy and Little Sis, I couldn't tell you who has read me. I don't plan to come out to Theía and Theío on this research and writing trip. Perhaps if The Doctor was with me, I would've felt compelled to introduce him to them. If The Doctor was the marrying kind, I'd invite Theía and Theío to our wedding. I don't feel it's important to share my sexuality or relationship status with Theía and Theío without occasion, without The Doctor here with me, without a wedding invitation or a wedding band on the ring finger of my left hand.

Common Root

Is Cyprus my motherland? My mother's land? When I've asked Mummy how she defines her identity in her own words, I've received multiple answers, variations on a theme of two islands.

'British.' 'British Cypriot.' 'Greek Cypriot.' 'British of Greek Cypriot heritage.'

Cyprus has been in flux for Mummy and, therefore, for me. It's been four years and four months since I was last here in Cyprus. It's been over a decade since I was last in Jamaica.

I had this realisation a few months ago when the Jamaican Poet Laureate Olive Senior was visiting London and I asked her what changes had happened in Jamaica since I was last there. I'd hoped she might tell me of developments in LGBTQ+ equality. Instead, she talked about the roads. She told me that the hill and gulley roads of Jamaica were less favoured by drivers now owing to new motorways. Flattening and limiting one's experience of the landscape. You were set apart from nature when driving through the island.

In my memories of Jamaica, we drove on winding roads, surrounded by lush green trees, the air conditioning blasting as it was unsafe to have your windows down or even to stop at traffic lights if you could avoid it because you could be carjacked by people waiting behind those trees with guns or machetes. I also remember how drivers flashed their headlights to warn other drivers of police cars around the corner waiting to catch them speeding. When we got into a car in Jamaica my body tensed up at the thought of police and thieves. I was terrified for these reasons and others during both my holidays to Jamaica in 2008 and 2011. Jamaican Uncle paid both times. I felt equal parts disappointment and relief that my dad didn't join us and the rest of my Jamaican family on either holiday.

I find a photo of me in 2008 on my first holiday to Jamaica standing in the middle of Dunn's River Falls, a famous waterfall near Ochi, or Ocho Rios, a port town on the north coast of Jamaica, its name Spanish for 'eight rivers'. I waded into the waterfall, terrified I'd slip on the smooth rocks, crack my head open and be washed downstream. In the photo I'm masking my fear with my smile, and a smiling aunt has her arm around me. She models a red tunic dress over her swimwear. Her hair is in protective braids. I have a small afro and I'm bare chested in blue swimming trunks. My stomach is flat and there's a V-shaped cut at my waistline. There's a thin 'happy trail' of hair from my belly button to my waistband. I look at this photo of myself a few months shy of twenty-four and think, he looks incredible, but he didn't feel it. He didn't feel body confident. He didn't feel confident in any way.

I was unsure of how to move my body. I was told not to walk too fast or else I'd look like a tourist and be targeted by locals trying to sell me things or rob me. I was also conscious that I wanted to appear straight and was mindful of the natural spring of my step and sway of my hips just as I'd been at Notting Hill Carnival back home in London. My true nature wasn't welcomed in Jamaica, so I kept my true nature captive. Same-sex sexual activity is illegal in Jamaica, so I wasn't hooking up with anyone.

Men in brightly coloured string vests caught my eye more than topless men – string vests felt like a tease and piqued my curiosity – but I kept my gaze in check even when I was wearing sunglasses because I didn't want to be attacked for being a 'batty man'. I was convinced that I didn't get beaten up or killed because I focused on my own body and didn't look at anybody else for too long.

I was in my twenties, but I felt like a frightened little boy all over again. I didn't feel safe to be my grown-up queer self in Jamaica. I thought of the Brixton spoken word poetry scene where Black poets and audience members told me they respected me, that I was 'brave' for being Openly Gay. I thought there was no stopping me from coming out at every opportunity since I'd come out back home. I had two opportunities to come out to my Jamaica-based family and I didn't take either.

My UK-based Jamaican family with whom I went on holiday in 2008 and 2011 knew I was gay, but it wasn't a topic of conversation with our Jamaica-based family. My fear was palpable to my entire Jamaican family even if they didn't know what was at the root of it.

The root of the word 'fear' is from the Middle English 'fere', from the Old English 'fær' meaning 'calamity, sudden danger, peril, sudden attack'. Like Cyprus, Jamaica was also a place in flux for me. Despite being surrounded by abundant love from Granny and the rest of my Jamaican family, Jamaica was full of fear and shame for me.

We were in the lap of luxury at the Jamaican holiday resort: we went horse riding and used the eighteen-hole golf course. I wasn't a confident swimmer back then, so I didn't go swimming with dolphins, but when Cuz suggested he and I went on a jet ski together, I felt the fear and did it anyway. Once we had life vests on, I was sure I wouldn't drown. I was afraid but decided to view my fear as a rush of excitement. I embraced my excitement as I sat at the back of the jet ski with Cuz driving us out to sea.

Way out and halfway through our time, Cuz stopped the jet ski and asked me if I wanted to switch positions and drive for the remainder of our time. I appreciated him asking but I said it was fine, I was having a good time on the back, and I didn't want to make the jet ski unsteady when we were out so deep. We had life vests on, but I didn't want to add to the risk of falling in as we jostled to switch positions.

I'd got my swimming badges at primary school. I didn't remember being afraid of water when I was a little boy. What was at the root of this fear?

'You're a coward,' scolded my inner critic.

'Okay.' Cuz shrugged. He continued to drive the jet ski, revving the engine and cutting shapes in the water as I held him tight from behind. I had a great time despite my fear.

When we returned to the rest of our family on the beach Cuz told Granny that I'd been screaming and clinging to him for dear life. He told Granny that when he offered to let me drive the jet ski, I'd begun to panic and scream 'No! No! NO!' I was sure that's not what happened, but as Cuz told it and Granny believed it, I wondered if his retelling of our jet ski ride was closer to the truth.

'Don't worry, baby, you're safe now, you can stay here by my foot.' Granny laughed, then looked at me sympa-thetically. The expression made me feel small and lowly but strangely reassured me too. I'd happily stay by Granny's foot because she is the strongest root of my Jamaican family tree. I had no doubt Granny loved and accepted me, as she did all her children and grandchildren.

Because my mum and dad didn't marry, I saw my Cypriot

family and Jamaican family as separate family trees, but I was still part of both. They were both lush and abundant with love. Cuz stayed at Mummy's countless times when we were young. In the school holidays, if he stayed for more than two or three days, he'd begin to tease me. He'd find a sore spot and keep pushing until I cried, or we had a physical fight. Not punching or slapping, more like wrestling. It was an aggressive but loving form of play. Of physical touch.

I didn't want to hurt him. He didn't want to hurt me. Cuz and I exerted an equal and opposite force on the other's body, we entangled like the roots of a tree beneath the ground. I twisted and tugged my body free of the hands that held me only to throw myself back into the tangle and resume our playful embrace. When he had the upper hand, my loving Cuz would only release me if I tapped out, cried or went limp like a dead weight.

'Game Over.'

Cuz wouldn't stop unless I showed him one of the above signs of submission. It was fun until it wasn't. Maybe we could've played *Mortal Kombat* on my Sega Mega Drive instead, maybe we could've talked more, but what we felt for each other was best expressed through these wrestling matches. It was a love on the edge of pain; we toyed with submission and domination long before I discovered this could also be something sexual. To me it was just how it went down when I was alone with Cuz. Unlike playing *Mortal Kombat*, going toe-to-toe with Cuz prepared me for real altercations like my one-on-one schoolyard fight and that homophobic attack on the south bank of the Thames.

Cuz knew my physical and emotional pressure points. By the time of our first Jamaica holiday, we were both twenty-three and I'd grown out of reach of my Cuz's teasing. I didn't wrestle him with words or body. I didn't cry or lash out as he mockingly repeated Granny's words during the rest of our holiday, adopting Granny's strong Jamaican accent.

'You can stay here by my foot.' Cuz began to titter with the 't' of 'foot'.

I felt a knot in my stomach. Cuz was cartoonish. Laughing at me like Muttley from *Wacky Races*. He took pleasure in mocking me and, while it did irk me, I didn't take it personally. He was laughing at his version of me, a version of me he'd created in his mind and in the minds of our family.

A butterfly afraid to fly. I was afraid, but it had little to do with the jet ski and more to do with the homophobic culture of the country. Cuz and I were side by side when a young Jamaican woman flirted with me on the beach. She called me a 'shy guy' when I didn't respond to her advances. I was afraid to say anything to her in case my voice or body language gave away that I was gay. 'Shy guy' became another phrase Cuz used mockingly, sampling and remixing it with Granny's words.

'Shy guy, you can stay here by my foot-t-t-t-t. Shy guy. T-t-t-t. Shy guy.'

My memories of Jamaica are limited like a motorway missing most of the landscape. Flattening the nuance of my roots and culture. I had to be straightforward and straight acting. I was an actor playing a dulled-down version of me even though I wasn't on stage or in the spotlight.

I think of the many versions of me: an elevated version; a man-sized version; a more innocent version; an earlier version; the aged-up and worn-out version; an edited version; his version of me, a version of me he'd created in his mind and in the minds of our family; a dulled-down version.

I stayed silent to protect my true self. To hide my true

nature. My holidays in Jamaica may have been luxurious but they didn't feel safe. I couldn't meander queerly in Jamaica. I couldn't pause to take in the sights. I couldn't be my hill-and-gulley self.

I long to make new memories in Jamaica. Beyond family. Memories of friendship, of community, of celebration and of safety. When I think for too long of my holidays in Jamaica, I feel in danger of losing myself to memories that no longer serve me or my future of abundance and prosperity.

I think of my dreadlocks and how I cut them off when they no longer served me. I think of the 'SILENCE IS NOT GOLDEN' t-shirt I wore early in my spoken word poetry career. I think of how I've stayed silent in my private life to protect myself and my relationships. My silence weighed on my shoulders like a heavy cloak woven from threads of stigma, fear and shame.

I think of black feathers on my shoulders when I was in drag as The Black Flamingo. The Doctor's legs over my shoulders when I rooted into him and told him 'I love you' for the first time. I want to section off these memories behind the velvet rope in my mind, I want to protect their roots from the rot of shame.

While I've not come out to my family in Cyprus, I've not been afraid of strangers knowing I'm gay when I'm here. I've had sex with men in Cyprus, both Cypriot men and other holidaymakers, and I've informed women that I'm gay when I've felt they were making sexual advances towards me. Homosexual sex has been legal in Cyprus since 1998 and the age of consent was equalised to seventeen in 2002.

I don't regret not coming out to Yiayia and Bapou. I've justified it to myself with the rationale that I didn't have a boyfriend I wanted to introduce to them. But this was only true for one of them.

Bapou was dead by the time I met The Doctor. But I was still not ready to come out to Yiayia, so I told her I lived with 'a friend' in Glasgow. Shrouded language. An echo of the hand-me-down secrecy and shame of my queer lineage. Not coming out to Yiayia feels like a missed opportunity, it feels cowardly, like not taking the opportunity to drive the jet ski in Jamaica.

Remembering Jamaica, remembering I didn't come out to Yiayia and Bapou, disappoints my inner child, my mixed-race butterfly boy, who dreamed of being Openly and Unapologetically Gay Every Single Day since coming out at high school. That dream was rooted in my well-meaning but naïve reaction to oppression, a politic of identity, not reality or safety.

That dream no longer serves me. That dream is as dead and gone as my Tamagotchi. I don't have it any more, so it can't be reset with a bent out of shape paper clip.

To Keep My Roots

At the spoken word poetry event at BLEND in Limassol, The Athenian and I were greeted at the door by a black dog called Flow, the tail-wagging, strokeable grand marshal of our welcome parade. Flow the dog stood on his hind legs and I held his front legs and shook them like a double handshake.

Our next greeting was an equally warm human hug from Melissa Zanga, the 2022 Cyprus national poetry slam champion, who runs BLEND, an arts collective that hosts workshops, life drawing classes, improvisation theatre and more. Melissa's earthy energy reminded me of many friends back home in the UK. Melissa felt familiar. BLEND felt like home. A sanctuary. Melissa told us we could sit to perform unless we wanted to stand and move our bodies.

The mismatched chairs consisted of sofas, armchairs, dining chairs and white plastic garden chairs. When I sat on a sofa, Flow the dog jumped up beside me and turned in a tiny circle before settling with his head on my lap. As I ran my fingers through Flow's fur, I thought about his name: the flow of water, the lyrical flow of a poet or rapper. Flow's owner, Melissa, must've had both meanings in mind, living on an island and working with words. I thought of how I went with the flow in my career.

The Greek word for 'flow', 'roí', can mean 'flow' and 'flux'. Flow, the black dog, was in flux between multiple meanings. I was aware of how the Black Dog is used as a metaphor for melancholy and depression. But this black dog evoked the opposite feeling. Flow's joyful welcome at the door followed by the way he'd found his own way to be side by side on the sofa with me both uplifted and served to ground me in my body. I thought then of the flow of yoga and how my yoga practice has changed my relationship with my body and my mind.

I missed the quiet companionship of my pet corn snake Ben. The way his red-brown body would coil around my golden-brown arm, his black-and-white checkerboard stomach, his laps of my body, charming me, chasing his own tail. I remembered holding the limp dead weight of him and promising him I'd never get another pet, promising never again would I keep such a beautiful thing as my captive.

Will I ever break this promise? Yes, I probably will. The Doctor has told me he'd love us to get a puppy. As a freelance writer with a flexible schedule, walking this hypothetical puppy and taking it to vet appointments would be my responsibility. It could be good for my mental health, but I don't want to be forced: I want to make healthy choices for myself not for the sake of preventing a restless puppy from shredding rolls of toilet paper or whatever they'd find to chew and destroy: my notebooks, our council tax bill or The Doctor's *British Medical Journal*.

I'm sorry, Hypothetical Puppy, but I don't have the capacity to feed you and walk you and give you my undivided attention all day until The Doctor comes home from work and then have to share him with you. Or, even worse, what if The Doctor gives you more attention than me? I'm not immune to jealousy. But if I'm going to get jealous, I want to be jealous of human competitors for my boyfriend's attention and not a creation of my imagination.

Once the mismatched chairs at BLEND were full of people, the performances began. We took turns over several rounds to perform or read our work from a designated performance armchair with the best sightlines. After each reading there was time to respond in the form of questions or reflections about what the performance made us think or feel. We came from many different backgrounds and lived experiences; we were as mismatched as the chairs we sat on. I realised 'blending in' didn't have to be about seeming the same as those around you or becoming lost in a crowd; it could be the acceptance of difference.

At BLEND we 'blended in' in so much as we respected a variety of performances, questions and opinions. I shared poems old and new. I shared 'Rome Is Eternal' from my debut poetry collection and reflected on how important it was for me that I'd written this unapologetic and unashamed poem celebrating a random hook-up. The penny dropped for some that I was Cypriot when I shared 'I Come From', from *The Black Flamingo*, and 'No Ascension', from my second poetry collection, *There is (still) love here*, about Bapou's death and my adoption of Greek Orthodox mourning customs. They tilted their heads to look at me from another angle, some nodded, a couple whispered to one another. I'd not said I was Cypriot to begin with. I didn't introduce myself before reading because my name, biography and photo were on the event page where it was noted that The Athenian and I were special guests. I know not everyone would've seen the event page. Nonetheless, I enjoyed sharing poems without introduction. Someone asked me what my full heritage was. I told them Mummy's family were Cypriot and my dad's family were Jamaican, but both were born and raised in London, as was I.

In the taxi returning from Limassol to Nicosia, I told The Athenian of my experiences trying to find a home in London when I moved out of Mummy's. I listed a few of the flat shares. There was an attic room in Battersea above a Vietnamese restaurant. There was living with a fellow drag performer in Shepherd's Bush with a view of Grenfell Tower.

There was the queer flat share on the twelfth floor of a 44-storey tower in the Grade II-listed Barbican Estate with brutalist architecture, underfloor heating, panoramic views of central London and a 24-hour porter service. We paid extra for a weekly cleaner. My privileged views of London reminded me of Mariah Carey's views of New York from her penthouse apartment.

I viewed the Barbican flat during golden hour when the afternoon sun cast a golden light into the living-cum-dining room. I told the flatmates I could only afford to live there for a limited period of six months; it was my gift to myself. I'd reached a small savings milestone back then, but I'd not decided what I was saving for, so it became a pot I allowed myself to dip into on months when I didn't earn anything.

February and October were my top earning months, LGBT+ History Month and Black History Month, respectively. Making money was less of a worry. Making meaning was my priority.

My summers were typically spent in Cyprus; flights were affordable, and I didn't need money once I was there. Accommodation and food were provided by Yiayia and Bapou. The sun and sea were free, and so were the hours of reading and writing in Yiayia and Bapou's Larnaca garden. A refuge. A retreat. A sanctuary. I read novels by David Nicholls and Zadie Smith. I took books with parallel texts of Greek poetry with English translations. Bapou and

I would take turns to read them to each other. Me: the English. Him: the Greek.

I wrote the genesis of *The Black Flamingo* in Yiayia and Bapou's Larnaca garden on an April evening in 2015. I had a good run of visits like this to Cyprus in summer and spring, and even one Christmas, before Yiayia and Bapou died. Since then, each year has been different and difficult in its own way, but I revisit Yiayia and Bapou's Larnaca garden in my mind when I want to remind myself of the safety I felt in that heaven on Earth. A safety I also felt looking through Cypriot Uncle's telescope at heavenly bodies.

I thought of the central London flat Jamaican Uncle lived in before he started a family and moved to a west London detached house. It was important to live in the Barbican queer flat share. Not only for the exclusivity of the surroundings and views of central London. Not only because it was a stone's throw from the Grade I-listed Guildhall Art Gallery where a portrait of me by Ajamu X had hung for a limited period of time in 2013. But because the Barbican queer flat share was sex-positive and international, with Greek, Italian and Australian flatmates and their sexual partners coming and going at all hours, which meant I didn't feel ashamed when I brought men back to the flat and helped me to believe I can have queerness, luxury and safety in my life. One of the flatmates was in a gay hockey team and I'd come home to find the whole team in the living-cum-dining room: muscular men filled the sofa and every chair around the dining table. But wait. There were more men on the floor. It looked like a photoshoot for a charity fundraising calendar. It felt like something out of a dream, to be surrounded by all this eye candy without having to pay for the privilege.

I wouldn't have survived the fall from our twelfth-floor

Barbican balcony. I had the thought once or twice early on and for that reason I only went out on the balcony when I had a guest over whom I wanted to impress by showing off the view and in front of whom I knew I wouldn't jump. Living somewhere as expensive as the Barbican made me believe I could make my Black queer life work, that it was going to work out, that I was going to find a way, even if I wasn't where I wanted to be yet. It sounds capitalist, but I had to believe I could afford to prioritise my comfort and I didn't have to hide my queerness to do this.

I grew up working class, albeit with an abundance of cultural capital, and it's only recently I've found financial security. Before I met The Doctor, I was ready to leave London because I could afford much more elsewhere than what I could afford in London. If I wanted comfort, if I wanted a comfortable place to live, maybe London wasn't the place for me on my earnings.

Before I met The Doctor, I was ready to leave London and excited about it. I was looking at Brighton and Manchester: both cities with vibrant poetry and LGBTQ+ communities. Most poets would welcome me with open arms if I moved to their city. I've realised this by travelling on work trips abroad, like this research and writing trip, and living in Glasgow with The Doctor for three years.

Each year was different in Glasgow. Each year will be different in London. Routines and rituals have become more important to me in place of an annual cycle of work. This typically looks like practising Greek, meditation and yoga and other activities to give my freelance life some structure.

On Mondays, Wednesdays and Fridays, The Doctor and I go bouldering. On Tuesdays and Thursdays, we place our yoga mats side by side on the kitchen floor – the reverse of how we sleep in bed, so he's on my right and I'm on his left – to do a yoga class from YouTube before breakfast.

Wednesday and Friday afternoons I go to talking therapy and an LGBTQ+ mental health support group, respectively. I've taken to burning lavender incense and keeping the radio on when I'm home alone to fill the flat with smoke and sound like a Greek Orthodox church. I listen to certain podcasts and radio shows, dare I say it, religiously. It's a wonder I find time to write.

When I'm at home writing, I clean up the kitchen after every meal. If mugs and dishes have piled up in the kitchen, I take it as a sign of my disorganised mind and wavering mental health. I'll make a to-do list, go for a walk, phone a friend, blast some Whitney and dance around the flat. If I want to dance with someone who loves me, that someone can be me. Sometimes this is home: dancing on my own. I typically feel better after that and can clean up my mugs and dishes, if not the rest of life's messes. Clean dishes and surfaces and a swept floor give me a sense of accomplishment in a world where so much is out of my control.

Running is not part of our routine but I'm still keen on it despite my runner's knee, so we run from time to time, and I'm prepared with an ice pack in the freezer for the pain that follows. The Doctor and I are both drawn to the bodies of water that snake through our neighbourhoods. In Glasgow, we ran beside the White Cart Water. In London, we run along the Regent's Canal.

In lockdown in Glasgow the routine that buoyed me most of all was when The Doctor cut my hair fortnightly in the communal garden behind our flat – this garden was my sanctuary during lockdown – it reminded me of Yiayia cutting Bapou's hair in their northwest London garden. Home hair appointments with The Doctor in Glasgow made it feel even more like home, not only because it reminded me of Yiayia and Bapou, but also because it reminded me of Mummy plaiting my afro into canerows and my Black and mixed-race friends at university who would twist my dreadlocks with beeswax to keep my roots neat.

These memories of home, of closeness and care, taught me how to receive love through my body. Home is a feeling; perhaps it's a choice of closeness and care, perhaps it's a community formed around shared interests and identities. Home can be many things for someone as privileged as me.

I could live anywhere in the UK and, with some paper-work and money, many places around the world. Sadly, that's not the case for all people. I don't take the privilege of travelling and finding community for granted, nor do I take my memories of past homes for granted either. I want to give my memories of past homes Grade I-listed status like buildings of exceptional interest on the palm tree-lined boulevard of my mind.

To Plant Roots

No one was wearing a seatbelt. On the Intercity bus from Nicosia to Larnaca, signs above the front window informed me that this bus held forty-nine seated passengers, none standing and no wheelchairs, no eating or drinking, no smoking and seatbelts must be worn.

I didn't see a sign for face masks, but everyone was wearing one. It surprised me that everyone was wearing a face mask since they'd been all but abandoned on public transport back home in London. I wore a new rainbow-coloured face mask, which was a gift from my nieces the last time I saw them. Mummy told me they picked it out themselves and asked her to buy it for me.

Stop by stop, Black and brown people filled the bus. None of whom gave off any tourist vibes. I suspected this would be the case. I wasn't necessarily glad to have this confirmed because I didn't know what it was like to live in Cyprus as a Black or brown person. A Black family of two adults and two children boarded the bus and separated to sit in front and behind me.

The little girl with a pink bow in her hair and gold studs in her pierced ears was in her mother's arms and looked longingly over her mother's shoulder, at her father behind me. The little boy stood backwards on his seat. I regarded his peppercorn hair, his runny nose and his big brown eyes, while he looked quizzically at me. I decided to turn around to ask the father if he wanted to swap seats with me but, as I turned, he began to speak on his mobile phone.

'Hello. I am the African man that came to see you about my wife . . .' he began. Perhaps he chose to sit separately from his children to make this important phone call. I looked past him and saw there were many free seats behind him and, if this family wanted to sit together, they could have sat back there. I couldn't help but hear that his phone call was about his wife's immigration status and an appointment they had in Larnaca. Paperwork and money. This family wanted to plant roots here in Cyprus.

After more Black and brown passengers boarded at the next stop, The Bus Driver left the door open and turned off the engine. He marched down the aisle; my body tensed as he stopped directly beside me. He addressed the divided family around me. He told them they had to get off the bus because they weren't wearing face masks. He ranted about police checks in Larnaca for face masks and seatbelts. He stressed that he'd be fined and could lose his licence if people weren't wearing face masks.

'Please,' the African man said, 'I have two children.'

'I have five children,' The Bus Driver said. 'I can't afford to lose my licence for you.'

The other passengers passed the family spare face masks and they put them on.

'We have masks now, you can drive,' said The African Man.

The Bus Driver wasn't satisfied. He refused to be undermined by the goodwill of the other passengers.

'You make me stressed. I cannot drive until you leave the bus,' declared The Bus Driver loudly. 'You will make everyone wait here until you leave the bus.' Was The Bus Driver trying to turn the other passengers against the family?

'But we have masks now, so you can drive. What's your problem?' asked The African Man.

'YOU ARE MY PROBLEM!' The Bus Driver yelled. 'I am the captain of this ship, and you will do as I say.'

'You are racist,' accused The African Man.

There was a collective groan from other passengers on the bus. We wished The African Man hadn't said this.

'You call me this? You call me racist?' The Bus Driver threw his hands in the air. 'I will not drive. You get off my bus now or I call the police to take you off.'

I thought of my great-uncle, Theío, who used to be a policeman here and I wondered how he would've handled this situation had he received such a call. Though I knew I wouldn't ask him when I saw him later.

A friend's mum had worked for the police. I'd dated a man who worked for the police. I tried to separate a person from their profession. This was not always possible. Doctors and the police take an oath. Their profession is intertwined with their character and integrity and lifestyle. The police I'd met socially tended to avoid talking about their jobs, perhaps owing to social stigma or perhaps owing to a level of trauma or even shame about what they've seen or done.

The policeman I'd dated had told me he worked in Westminster. I took this to mean he worked at the Houses of Parliament, somewhere I'd been invited to on a number of occasions, including to perform a poem I'd written to commemorate the life and death of Nelson Mandela. It wasn't until a few dates in that my policeman told me what his job was. He told me he kept his profession private until a few dates in because most men he'd met on the gay scene weren't into policemen. He also told me that he wasn't out as gay to his work colleagues because he heard a lot of homophobic banter bandied about at work. He sounded as if he was caught between two worlds. A closeted policeman at work and an out gay man in the clubs and on the hook-up apps. I told him it was my goal since coming out at high school to be Openly and Unapologetically Gay Every Single Day. He told me he was out on a need-to-know basis.

The Bus Driver marched off. He stopped a few paces in front of the bus, reached into his pocket for a packet of cigarettes. I thought of Bapou. The Bus Driver made dramatic gestures as he spoke and blew puffs of cigarette smoke. The other passengers slowly but surely, sigá-sigá, talked him down from his anger and anxiety.

I wondered if this was a regular occurrence on these buses. I wondered if volatile bus drivers and unmasked racial prejudice were something those other passengers were accustomed to. I felt a dull pain at the front of my left knee, my runner's knee, which seemingly isn't restricted to running; in recent years it flares up when I sit in one position for too long. I didn't dare stand to stretch. I was glued to my seat. Once he finished his cigarette, The Bus Driver returned to the driver's seat. He turned on the engine, shut the door and drove onwards towards Larnaca without another word.

'You did nothing. You're a coward. You're pathetic,' scolded my inner critic. This voice in my head was competing with the dull pain at the front of my left knee.

'You did *nothing*.' The bus was so quiet I was certain everyone could hear my inner critic on repeat.

'You're a *coward*.' The bus was so quiet I was certain everyone could hear my left knee click when I straightened it out into the aisle.

'You're *pathetic*.' The bus was so quiet now that all I could think to do was to take out my mobile phone, open the Notes app and take note of what had happened.

I boarded this bus at its first stop, and I disembarked at

its last. Finikoudes beach was as I remembered: a sandy palm tree-lined beach, kiosks selling iced coffee, a slow flow of cars and mopeds on the one-way road towards the medieval castle of Larnaca, supposedly built in the Middle Ages and fortified during the Ottoman rule. Some smaller restaurants might have changed but there was McDonald's and KFC and there was the children's play area next to Hobo's café and restaurant, where I was to meet my Cypriot aunt in two hours. The January sun was an LED light: bright but not warming.

I remembered all the times I'd been to these places with Mummy and Little Sis over the decades and most recently with my nieces.

I remembered being single in Cyprus before my nieces were born and using a hook-up app to meet men.

I remembered the two Israeli men I had a threesome with in their seafront holiday apartment.

I remembered the older Cypriot man with an impressive art collection in his palatial seafront residence with whom I didn't have sex but chatted for several hours.

I remembered how afterwards, sex or no sex, I blocked them on the app as soon as I left because I was ashamed of myself for sneaking away from family holidays to meet men.

I remembered before the hook-up apps, when that random older man swam over and masturbated me there in the Mediterranean Sea. I felt like a man in that moment, but I wasn't.

I can't have been that young, I reassured myself. *I came to Cyprus for the first time when I was fifteen. So, I must've been in my late teens.*

I forgave myself for not remembering what age I was. I thought I'd forgiven myself for that 'incident' decades ago. I thought of it as an 'incident' rather than a sexual assault.

Because I didn't want there to have been so many sexual assaults.

Because I didn't say 'No', but he didn't ask before he touched me.

Because I didn't say 'Stop', but I didn't say anything to encourage him either.

'You must've smiled at him,' said my inner critic.

I'd not forgiven myself for this incident.

I felt a knot in my stomach as I looked out at the sea, and the sea looked back at me. I felt ashamed of my navel gazing. The Mediterranean Sea knew untold horrors. The International Organization for Migration recorded 2,411 migrant deaths and disappearances in the whole of Mediterranean Sea in 2022.

It was a sunny day, but the sea was rough; white bronco waves galloped towards the shore, and a couple of wind-swept people zipped up their jackets as they marched past me. There was a solo black backpack on the sand, which signified a swimmer was out there in the sea somewhere. I couldn't see them. There were lifeguards on duty in their towers. I trusted they were watching out for this person.

I spotted a sailboat in the distance and remembered my long-lost *Blue Peter* badge and going sailing at primary school and someone yelling 'man the rigging' and having to put my whole body into pulling a rope. I felt like a man in that moment, but I wasn't.

I wondered if any lifeguards had seen what that random older man did when I was in my late teens. I wondered if that random older man made a habit of swimming up to young men and masturbating them. I wondered if I had made myself easy prey for this predator of Finikoudes beach. If he was a shark, did that make me a seal? A tasty meal?

'Whether you wanted it or not, you've got to forgive yourself,' said my inner cheerleader.

On that January day on that sandy beach in Larnaca, I thought of how I couldn't relax in Jamaica.

I thought of how I couldn't relax when I tried to sit and meditate on the pebble beach in Brighton. If I didn't recognise someone approaching me on Brighton beach, I'd wonder if they were a friend from university, someone trying to buy drugs from me, or a man from the gay sauna.

I thought of frequenting the gay sauna. 'SHAME' ran through my core indelibly. Could I dissolve this inner pillar of 'SHAME' and remain intact, or would 'SHAME' be part of me until the day I died?

Into my multicoloured backpack I'd packed blue swimming trunks, a gift from The Doctor, and a white towel, borrowed from the Nicosia hotel.

It was January but I knew swimming would be a possibility. I knew the cold water would be good for my runner's knee. I had two hours free before I was meeting my aunt for lunch. We'd go to Bapou's grave, visit Yiayia and Bapou's Larnaca house for the final time before it was sold and visit my great-aunt and uncle for coffee and cake late in the afternoon. I could either sit somewhere and write or trust my instincts and go for a swim in the Mediterranean.

The Doctor and I have swum in many cold lochs, rivers, seas and oceans over three years of living in Scotland. I'd felt the rush of standing under waterfalls and immersing myself in fairy pools, so when I got the opportunity to safely enter cold water, I took it.

I love outdoor swimming. I'm not the strongest swimmer but I'm no longer afraid of water. I didn't need The Doctor to be there with me to take the plunge, but I acknowledge The Doctor for helping me to love and trust the water, for helping me to love and trust myself.

I thought of how The Doctor told me he'd been wearing

the pyjamas I'd left under my pillow because he missed me, and those pyjamas smelled of me. I thought of how missing each other helps us appreciate each other.

I made my way to the tideline, rolled up my light blue Levi's, took off my black Nike trainers and rainbow-coloured socks. I stepped in, and a wave lapped over my bare toes, followed by another up to my ankles. Imagine a bath you'd forgotten for hours and had gone cold but there was still warmth in there. A tepid body of water, like Bapou's still-warm dead body.

The one time we came to Cyprus for Christmas, after dinner we marched the length of Finikoudes beach from the marina to the medieval castle. None of my family wanted to swim.

'You must be joking!' 'It's freezing!' Echoes of their voices in the wind.

Maybe I was brave enough to dip my toes in that Christmas, but I can't be sure.

As I got out of my clothes and into my swimming trunks, I thought of Scotland, swimming off the coast of the Outer Hebrides and the Isle of Arran as well as in Loch Lomond with The Doctor. I was excited to tell him about this before I'd even done it. He's the first person I want to tell of my achievements. I felt a rush of excitement as I faced the sea and the sea faced me.

I set down my backpack and trainers a few paces from the tideline, rainbow socks peeking out. I was doing this as my own man. I wanted to be my own knight in shining armour, my own Prince Charming. Even though I had come on this research and writing trip with The Athenian, I was glad neither he nor The Doctor were with me on Finikoudes beach.

There was someone I needed to meet in the sea. It wasn't the owner of the black backpack who must've still been somewhere in the waves, nor was it the random older man who swam over and masturbated me when I was in my late teens. I waded into the waves in search of my inner child, to let him know it was safe to be alone in the sea, stripped back and unaccompanied.

The waves were strong, but I'd felt stronger ones when surfing with The Doctor in Newquay last October. With the index finger of my left hand, I'd poked my pot belly. I'd chuckled to myself about how I looked like a seal or a selkie snugly squeezed into the second skin of my wetsuit.

In London last Christmas, Niece Two came to me on the sofa and climbed onto my lap.

'You're fat,' she said, matter-of-factly, as she poked my pot belly.

'I'm not fat. I've just eaten,' was my kneejerk reaction. I didn't laugh like Bapou used to.

I don't see myself as fat. I see myself as fit and flexible. There's not a crack, crevice or fold on my body I can't reach. My body mass index may read as 'obese', but I'm not worried because I know I've made every effort to live a healthier life in recent years and intend to continue on this path.

In Newquay last October, our surf instructor was slim, toned and sexy. His sun-bleached, golden-brown curls were his crowning glory. If a threesome with The Doctor had been on the cards, I'd have been up for it.

'This reminds me of yoga!' I told the surf instructor as he took us through the moves to get from flat on our bellies on the board to standing up riding a wave.

'Plank to baby cobra to lizard and jump up into warrior two,' I told myself, connecting his instructions to movements my body already knew.

Once we'd completed the safety talk and warm-up exercises on Fistral beach, I wasn't afraid, I was so excited to get in. I lay on the deck of the board and held the rails until the right waves came rushing towards us. I paddled furiously to get up to speed and popped up into fighting stance.

When I was thrown from the board, which was often, I put one hand to the crown of my head and the other to the back of my neck so as not to get hit by the fins on the underside of the board, as I'd learned in the safety talk. I felt safe. I felt unlimited when I was thrown from the board and plunged in. I didn't panic. I knew how to recover. I felt unlimited when I managed to stand on the board and ride my first wave all the way back to Fistral beach.

In Larnaca I wasn't wearing a wetsuit, I wasn't attached to a surfboard, and I wasn't trying to catch a wave. Even without a wetsuit, I'm insulated like a seal by my body's fat. The sea wasn't as rough as it looked from the shore. I swam out to a comfortable depth and then began swimming parallel to Finikoudes beach in the direction of the medieval castle. The dull pain at the front of my left knee had already faded.

I swim breaststroke. When I try front crawl or butterfly, I feel like I'm forcing my body to do something it's not ready for. I know swimming more often, doing weights and pull-ups would help my stamina and strength. But, for now, I'm happy I can stay afloat and move through water in a way that suits my current capabilities and comfort level. Breaststroke is slow and steady, not too taxing for me. It's not flash. It doesn't make a splash. The patient and purposeful work of this stroke happens beneath the surface.

The waves were pushing me towards the shore, so I decided to stop swimming and floated on my back. My arms and legs outstretched. My inflatable belly a floatation device. When I breathed in deeply my body rose higher; when I breathed out, I sagged a little in the middle but stayed afloat.

Mummy floated on the surface of the water on our holidays here, but she couldn't get me to relax enough in the water to teach me how it was done. With her hands underneath me in the water, my body would stiffen, and I'd need to stand and regain my composure before trying and failing again.

In 2017 a swimming enthusiast friend took me to a Brixton swimming pool to teach me how to float, but I panicked in the pool and had to leave. The first time I successfully floated without assistance was in the Atlantic Ocean on our camper van trip in the Outer Hebrides last August. There was nothing to do other than relax and trust my body, trust the ocean.

It was too heavy for me to fathom that an estimated two million people – who were enslaved and forced to leave Africa – died in the Middle Passage being transported in boats across the Atlantic Ocean, let alone the horrors faced by an estimated ten to eleven million enslaved people who survived the Middle Passage. I'm not a historian. I'll rarely look back before the sixties when my parents were born or the thirties when my grandparents were born.

The Doctor watched me proudly. He felt like family. When I'd found a steady state on the surface, he swam to me and floated beside me. We held hands and floated side by side like sleeping sea otters. Not my lifeline, my life partner. Not only did I trust the ocean, I trusted The Doctor, and he trusted me not to panic and pull him down with me.

Carrying more weight, more mass than The Doctor, I could stay in cold water for longer than him. I was more confident in open water since floating in the Atlantic Ocean and since our surfing lesson in Newquay. The Doctor and I had swum in lochs, leisure centre pools and lidos. Yoga and meditation had helped me find trust for my body and surroundings; the vulnerability of happy baby, the balance of tree, the relaxation of child's pose, the surrender of savasana or corpse: the pose in which I was floating.

The Mediterranean could take my weight. The sea was neither for me nor against me. The sea was ambivalent. Our relationship was ambiguous. I had to trust it like I had to trust myself.

I lay on my back buoyed by the salt in the sea. I lay down my burdens on this body of water. I relaxed as I floated on my back in the open water, the waves pushing me towards Finikoudes beach. Towards the open palms of its tall trees. Towards the rest of my life. I felt safe to close my eyes for a moment and let my mind drift. I thought of the waves of grief in my life for Yiayia and Bapou. I thought of my flashbacks and waves of anger since the rape, a tidal force in my life.

While I didn't see my risky sex as brave or sex for sport as healthy, I no longer blamed myself for the sexual assaults I'd survived. I saw it like this: I could let myself sink in self-blame and self-pity or I could float and swim in this open water full of ambiguity.

I remembered Cypriot Uncle's telescope and how at night we looked up at the moon, planets and stars, heavenly bodies I knew were there beyond daytime blue. I imagined that if I breathed in deep enough, I'd lift off, drift off above Larnaca, above Cyprus, higher and higher, like a hot air balloon. I let out a sigh. My midriff sagged, but I stayed afloat.

I am both the sea and the sky, I thought.

I chuckled at the thought of myself as a hot air balloon floating above the salty Mediterranean Sea, and something stirred within me. I didn't need to look for him, my inner child, my mixed-race butterfly boy. I felt him uncurl and spread himself within me where he'd been hiding for decades, awaiting safety. I'd kept him to myself. I'd hidden him. Was he the boy who pilfered paper clips or the boy who wrote the petition? Was he the boy who lost his denim jacket or the boy who once believed in ghosts?

Time folded in on itself.

A butterfly too weak to fly can't go back to being a cater-pillar. I saw myself floating, arms and legs outstretched testing my wingspan. I felt weightlessness. The grey hairs in my beard turned brown again, then my beard disappeared. My afro grew back rapidly spreading from its roots; it covered the surface of the water around my head, a black halo no one could touch. My belly became flat. My 'missing piece' and other tattoos faded and disappeared. I saw my inner child, my mixed-race butterfly boy, baptised at fifteen, in gay saunas in his late teens and twenties, there in Larnaca at thirty-eight, one and the same person, superimposed onto himself.

My 38-year-old body was a cocoon or second skin, my inner child, my mixed-race butterfly boy, was trapped within. I felt sad for him to be trapped inside me. The armour we wear in public can be a cocoon that allows us to transform in private, but only if we one day shed our armour and emerge from our cocoon. This is easier said than done. Especially if we fear that when we emerge, our loved ones will no longer recognise us.

I was full of fear and shame.

My 38-year-old body was a snakeskin my inner child couldn't shed. My inner child felt ashamed of his appetites, his needs and desires, which were now my appetites, my needs and desires. He felt ashamed of what Mummy might've seen on that desktop computer, which is now my compulsion to clear my internet search history daily. Every day a chance to repent or a choice to sin again.

My inner child felt ashamed of how many men had access to him. These men were a paper clip chain to be kept hidden. He believed gay sex was sinful and shameful. Because of this, the majority of sex I had was in secret. Because of this, the times I was sexually assaulted were long-held secrets too.

My inner child felt ashamed these men had taken advantage of him. He felt ashamed for not saying no, which I know isn't enough to stop some people. He felt ashamed of not speaking up more, which is why I speak up for us both.

My inner child, my mixed-race butterfly boy, wasn't made of shame, he was made of love. But he was confused. He didn't understand who he was. I called myself Black and queer, but he saw himself as mixed-race and gay. He didn't know we could be all of those things. He didn't know that he was still me and I was still him.

How could I be both this timid mixed-race butterfly boy and the bold black flamingo? Because The Black Flamingo is a character, a persona or alter ego I hide behind, and my mixed-race butterfly boy is who I was hiding. Boy, not buoy. Man, not anchor. I could float and swim in this open water full of ambiguity.

I wanted to give my inner child, my mixed-race butterfly boy, his fairy-tale ending. I wanted him to fly free of me, wild and free, healed and happy, but he was still me and I was still in the process of healing him. I believe I will heal him. Sigá-sigá, slowly but surely.

The word 'yoga' comes from the Sanskrit 'yuj', 'to unify'. My inner child, inner critic, inner cheerleader and I floated together, in union, on the surface of the water, breathing with the ebb and flow of the waves. Waves of time, emotion and memory held me, my multiple selves, afloat, allowing us to merge. Just like my British, Cypriot and Jamaican identities merge, variations on a theme of three islands, when I'm with my family, my friends and The Doctor, and all those who love and accept me unconditionally as I am, without question, without doubt.

Buried

My Cypriot aunt drove me to the cemetery to pay my respects to Bapou. I thought of how 'cemetery' in Greek, 'koimitírion', means 'sleeping place' when I saw a ginger cat curled on a bench at the entrance to the cemetery that stands atop a hill with views over Larnaca and Aradippou. I thought of Little Bapou in Aradippou being hit for writing with his left hand. I thought of Bapou telling me, 'You are lucky!'

'I'm lucky to be alive,' I thought. I'd felt over the hill at thirty-one and past my prime at thirty-three. At thirty-eight in a cemetery atop a hill, as I walked past graves of children and adults younger than me and towards my grandfather, imagining living into my eighties like him, I did feel lucky. I'd received many bouquets of fresh flowers from my boyfriend and others, and I'd been alive to smell them. The flowers at these graves were plastic bouquets. The flowers at Bapou's grave were orange and white and looked like a bunch of emoji flowers, unnatural but understandably practical.

My aunt, who lives in Larnaca, told me she visits Bapou's grave regularly but especially on important days such as Bapou's birthday and his name day, St George's Day. I knew St George as the patron saint of England, but he has a long list of patronages throughout the world. The headstone of

Bapou's grave is a marble structure, more like a mantelpiece with a glass-fronted cabinet. Inside the cabinet, on either side of a silver-clad icon of St George on horseback slaying a dragon with a spear, were two framed photos.

Photo one was young George, before he was my grandfather, probably in his twenties, handsome, serious-looking, with a full head of hair combed back. He wore a white shirt, black tie, black suit jacket; this was a black-and-white photo that had been colourised. This was the young man who left Cyprus.

In living colour, photo two was Bapou as I remembered him, older, with a round face and a cheeky smile, sat in his northwest London garden, the sun shining down on his balding crown. He wore a white shirt, open collared, and a casual brown jacket. This was the older man who returned to Cyprus.

Young serious George. Silver-clad Saint George. Older smiley Bapou. Three images. There was only one Bapou: the body of my grandfather buried six feet under, repatriated by Cypriot soil.

This was supposed to be a family grave, the heartland of my Cypriot family. Yiayia was supposed to be buried here with Bapou, but Mummy and her siblings decided to bury Yiayia in London simply because Yiayia had died in London. My Cypriot uncle visits Yiayia's grave in London weekly. Despite living in London now, I haven't returned to Yiayia's grave since her funeral last May. I don't think Yiayia would mind. Unorthodox Yiayia will for ever be wearing a bright floral summer dress in my mind.

When I die, I want to be buried in London like Yiayia. But if I were to be cremated, I'd want my ashes scattered in the Atlantic Ocean and Mediterranean Sea. That said, I hope to return to Cyprus soon and often, with The Doctor, with Mummy, with Little Sis and my nieces, and on my own. I hope to make many more memories across this ancient island. My experience of Cyprus need not be limited to one family, one house, one city or one side. And if I'm being honest, which I am, I hope that when I'm gone there'll be Cypriots who remember me as one of their own.

Network of Roots

There was an abundance of life outside. Plants grew from cracks in the driveway, at the side of the house a once-small orange tree entangled with a tall palm tree. I wanted to call it Yiayia and Bapou's orange tree but, since they were gone, no one had been tending to their Larnaca garden and the orange tree, belonged to itself, as did the palm tree and all the other plants in this abandoned garden. It was embarrassingly lush, more alive than ever, with no regard whatsoever for Yiayia and Bapou's deaths.

I'd imagined the Larnaca garden would die when Bapou did, but the orange tree and palm tree were thriving in this garden of wild abandon. The orange tree had grown up and around the palm tree to take advantage of its height and make itself as tall as the house. If you'd so wished, you could've picked oranges from that upstairs window.

As I looked up, I felt a sinking feeling. I contemplated how these trees might also be entangled underground, connected by a network of roots and mycorrhizal fungi in the soil, communicating and cooperating in ways humans fail to fathom. Yiayia and Bapou's Larnaca house sat unoccupied for ten months while Mummy and her siblings decided whether to sell it. They couldn't decide whether to arrange a house clearance, what to keep, if anything, and whether they could do anything until everyone had returned to the house for one last visit. This garden without its gardener, this unoccupied house, was no longer the sanctuary it once was. It was a puzzle, a problem to be solved.

I only know a citrus tree by its fruit and a palm tree by its fronds. Even though I watched Bapou tend his gardens here in Larnaca and in northwest London, I didn't know what most of the plants were. What mattered most was time with him, be that in his garden or going 'for a walk' to the corner shop.

With all the overgrowth in the Larnaca garden, I'd half expected it to have taken over the inside of the house, but there were no plants inside. There was no natural light, the blinds were closed, the air was stale. It felt unliveable, not a family home or a holiday home. It was no kind of home. In the sala, white sheets draped over the sofas made them ghosts of their former selves. White mould had grown up the walls, chunks of plaster crumbled off. Dead cockroaches and little black specks on each surface below waist height.

'Not even cockroaches can live here,' my aunt quipped glibly.

I'd been sure I wanted to see this house one last time and perhaps take a keepsake. I'd kept Bapou's watch and prayer beads when he died. Needing neither since I don't wear a watch or pray.

I felt it rise in me like a tide, that instinct to take something I didn't need. I'd thought maybe I'd want to take Bapou's Tavli set this time to add to my personal British Museum. I took the wooden box down from the bookcase, placed it on the coffee table and opened it and saw the round black and white pieces, the two boards with faded bars. I didn't want to play this Tavli set. It would probably sit on my own bookcase until the day I died and then my nieces would have to decide if they wanted to keep it. Would that make this board game a family heirloom?

I remembered a conversation with my nieces two weeks prior at the British Museum.

'Why did they dig them up?' Niece One asked, pointing at an Egyptian mummy behind glass.

'Can we dig up Big Yiayia?' Niece Two asked, not giving me the chance to answer her sister.

'No,' I said as I crouched to their level, 'we can't dig up Big Yiayia. And I think these mummies should've been left where they were in Egypt.'

'Where's the queen buried?' asked Niece Two.

'She's buried with her husband, Prince Philip, in Saint George's Chapel at Windsor Castle.'

I couldn't help but think of Yiayia and Bapou buried separately – one in London, the other in Larnaca.

'Why didn't God save the queen?' asked Niece Two.

At Yiayia and Bapou's Larnaca house, that memory – and my instinct to take something – subsided. I had a Tavli set back home in London. It was enough for me to see Bapou's one last time, now I could keep it in my mind. I shut Bapou's wooden box and put it back on the bookcase. There were no books I wanted. There were no framed photos Mummy didn't already have copies of back home in London. I had access to everything I wanted. There was nothing I wanted to take home from that house or garden, not a book or board game, not a photo or fruit. Mummy, me, Little Sis, Nieces One and Two are the fruit of Yiayia and Bapou.

Crown to Root

Tracks for a new chairlift snaked the stairs. My Cypriot aunt and I had been buzzed into Theía and Theío's building. They lived in the upstairs flat while their daughter and grandchildren lived on the ground floor.

'Hello?' my aunt called up the stairs.

'Hello, my dears,' Theía said. 'Ella, come, we're up here.'

We climbed the stairs to our glamorous film-star-like relatives. Their home boasts many photos of them when they were young, posing like a Hollywood poster, like Humphrey Bogart and Ingrid Bergman in *Casablanca*. Theía and Theío's had been a great love story. They were affectionate with one another. They spoke kindly to each other. I admired them. I felt guilty comparing them to Yiayia and Bapou, who hadn't seemed as happy together.

I saw Theía and Theío for one afternoon coffee on each visit to Cyprus. I'd be with Mummy and Little Sis and last time with my nieces as well. We'd bring pastries from Zorbas bakery. Theía made Cyprus coffee on the stove. I took my coffee 'metrios', medium, one teaspoon of sugar added while the coffee was on the stove.

'Hello, Dean!' Theío used to be taller. He held himself upright using his new walking stick. He was a little crumpled, not only his clothes but his whole person.

'Hello, Theío!' I threw my arms open and stepped into

his embrace. His hug was strong and sturdy and, as always, he kissed me on both cheeks. A perfect hello.

I felt a flutter in my belly. Theío was the only man in my family, in my life, who kissed me on both cheeks. This man's affection had been the purest I'd known. Nothing had ever tainted it. I'd not heard a bad word said of Theío. I'd not seen him be anything but gentle and loving.

Theío used to be a policeman. I didn't ask about his career. I can't attest to what Theío was like as a policeman. I can't attest to what Theío was like as a brother to Yiayia, since I rarely saw them together.

Yiayia didn't greet me with coffee or kisses. She greeted me with tea and biscuits. But for as long as I could remember, her brother, Theío, had hugged me and kissed me on both cheeks.

Physical touch must be one of Theío's top love languages, I thought.

Jamaican Uncle's top love languages are gifts and quality time. Before my nieces were born, I didn't consider an uncle's love half as much as I have in recent years. I loved Niece One from the moment Little Sis told me she was pregnant. I was as in love with the idea of her as I was afraid of the idea of us losing her. And this was before we'd lost Yiayia and Bapou.

A few days ago in Athens, I bought my nieces matching Evil Eye bracelets, for protection and tradition. I'm excited to return home to London soon and give them these gifts and spend quality time with them. Like my aunts and uncles have for me, I try to show up for my nieces all year round.

When I take my nieces out, I'm a hand-holding road-safety tyrant when crossing the road.

'Hold my hand.' 'Wait for the green man.' 'Look both ways.'

When we're safely in the park and they want to scale a climbing frame too big for them or the branches of a tall tree, I enjoy strategising with them about how it could be possible with a bit of help from their Uncle Dean. I help my nieces onto a climbing frame or into a tall tree, into the sky, from their perspective, to become taller than me. I love to help them push and surpass the limits of their bravery.

I've become braver over the past five years with The Doctor. I find activities such as hiking, mountain biking and surfing give me a rush of excitement and a sense of accomplishment. While I had a bike, rollerblades and a skateboard as a child, I didn't take any risks on them. I'd got my swimming badges at primary school, and I didn't remember being afraid of water when I was a little boy. I didn't understand why I didn't feel confident in water until The Doctor encouraged me to swim out of my depth. I'd been in sink-or-swim survival mode my whole life.

My bravery as a child was channelled into auditions and performances that gave me that rush of excitement and sense of accomplishment. My bravery at fifteen was asking out The Redhead. Even though he said no to me, I said yes when schoolmates asked me if I was gay. I may not have managed to be Openly and Unapologetically Gay Every Single Day from then on but, as an adult, I've displayed bravery in abundance. From persevering as a freelance writer to doing drag for the first time. From saying 'I love you' to The Doctor within the first month of meeting him to moving to a new city with him after a year and a half. From processing multiple sexual assaults to writing a book that shines a spotlight on them.

Theía was shrinking. Each time I saw her, she was squatter, a person made of play dough squashed by an invisible hand pressing upon her head.

'It's so good to see you, my dear.' She hugged me tightly and I could've rested my chin atop her head if I'd so wished.

This was how a real-life fairy tale ended, sigá-sigá, slowly but surely shrinking and crumpled like Theía and Theío. What a privilege it would be to reach this ripe old age and have a love like this.

With a squeeze I said, 'It's so good to see you too.'

As she did each time we visited, Theía apologised that we'd be having our coffee in the kitchen rather than the formal living-cum-dining room. I'd not seen this room in use. As we walked past, I glanced at the dining chairs and sofas I'd not sat on even once, let alone been surrounded in them by a gay hockey team like at the Barbican flat.

In the kitchen, I took my regular chair at the cluttered table and waited to be asked how I'll take my coffee.

'Metrios,' I said in Greek.

Theía nodded in approval.

'So, you've been to the cemetery to pay your respects to your Bapou?' she asked but continued, 'Your Bapou really loved you. Both of your grandparents did.'

'I know,' I said. Even though I could've said it in Greek: Xéro.

I looked from Theía, who was making our Cyprus coffee on the stove, to Theío who was sat directly across from me at the kitchen table.

'I'm so proud of you,' Theío said.

Was he proud because I'd come to visit Bapou's grave or was there another reason?

Words of affirmation must be Theío's other top love language, I thought.

'Thank you,' I said. Even though I could've said it in Greek: Efcharistó.

Theía set a coffee in front of me. An act of service.

I winced at the logo on the coffee cup that featured a

Black man in a hotel bellboy uniform. His thick lips and broad nose seemed overemphasised in monochrome. I'd not seen this logo for years and hadn't considered its racial stereotypes of a Black man being depicted in a service role.

'Thank you,' I said. I didn't want to turn such precious time into a conversation about race.

My aunt opened the cake box we'd brought with us and began to dish them out. Cheesy pastries and baklava. I chose one of each.

'How did your workshop go?' Theía asked.

'The workshop's tomorrow,' I said. 'But I performed at two open mic nights. One on Tuesday in Nicosia and one on Wednesday in Limassol.'

'And they went well?' asked Theía.

'Yes, they both went really well,' I said.

'I'm so proud of you,' Theío repeated.

'And he went to the north yesterday,' said my aunt.

I'd not planned to tell them.

'So, you crossed the border?' Theía asked me. 'How was it?'

All the words in my mind were loaded. I stayed silent.

'I won't show my passport to travel in my country,' Theío said, a hand to his heart as if that's where Cyprus was.

Then, Theía told me how in July 1974 she and Theío went to stay with Yiayia and Bapou who had lived in London since the sixties. Theía needed inner ear surgery and wanted it done by a specialist on Harley Street.

Theía told me Bapou called this her 'lucky ear' because it meant Theía and Theío weren't in Cyprus during the coup d'état, initiated by the Greek military junta, and Turkey's invasion and occupation of the north of the island.

Theío added that he worked with Bapou in a factory in London for a few months until it was safe for Theía and

Theío to return to Cyprus. 'They arrested my whole unit,' Theío said, speaking of his police colleagues.

I didn't want to ask any more. I fell silent; we all did.

I understood why my elders could only give me limited information about Cyprus in July 1974. They weren't there. Theía and Theío by chance. Yiayia and Bapou by choice.

Yiayia and Bapou didn't return to live in Cyprus until they were pensioners.

'So did you have your workshop in the buffer zone yesterday?' asked Theía.

'Óchi, eínai ávrio,' I said in Greek, to be clear.

Theía laughed and translated my words back, 'No, it's tomorrow.' She laughed again. 'Well done, my dear. Your Greek is getting better.'

Words of affirmation.

Greek is the most important love language here, I thought.

'He practises on an app,' my aunt said encouragingly.

I did practise Greek on an app. I also practised meditation on an app. I found my way with apps: Maps, Notes and hook-up apps.

I saw myself through Theío's eyes. 'I'm so proud of you,' he said for a third time.

I wondered whether Theío knew he'd said this three times or if he had dementia like his sister, Yiayia. I wondered how long I'd be back home in London before I received a call that Theío was in a critical condition in hospital. I thought of Bapou telling me, 'You are lucky.'

Since Bapou died I'd been so afraid of losing more loved ones. And yet last year when Yiayia was diagnosed with dementia and I knew death was the inevitable outcome of the disease, it still took me by surprise that she died so soon.

Theío might not have dementia. It could be that he's extremely proud of me. It could be both.

'You must do a reading here in Larnaca next time,' Theía

said. 'We'll be in the front row to support you.' She waved an invisible flag in the air to show me what their support would look like. I imagined a rainbow flag in her hand, even though I'd not come out to them.

'Yes, next time,' I said.

Time slowed.

I hoped to return with The Doctor to visit Theía and Theío for coffee and pastries next time. Theía and Theío are two of the strongest roots of my Cypriot family tree. They present the final opportunity for me to be accepted by the eldest living generation of my Cypriot family. I hope they're here next time. Losing Yiayia and Bapou has taught me I can't take my family or any of my loved ones for granted.

Love need not be limited by language or location. Love is a galaxy of uncharted planets and stars. Love is abundant, an unlimited resource.

Granny's abundant love is stalwart. Yiayia and Bapou's love was conditional and complicated for Mummy but became simpler for me. Love can be orthodox for some and unorthodox for others.

Love is at the root of my life. Love is the choice that saved my life and made my life worth living. I felt grateful to Theía and Theío, whose Hollywood-poster great love story inspired me to visualise what I could have in the future with The Doctor.

I thought again of Bapou saying, 'You are lucky.'

In my mind, I replied, 'It's not luck, Bapou, it's love, agápi mou.'

My love, my self-love, looked like a golden light that flowed into me from above, from crown to root, the light filled my core with pure love. Full of light. Full of life. Full of love.

Abundance. I'd practised this. I'd visualised it with the

help of that meditation app, but it hadn't felt like this before. I was awash with love. The love from above dissolved the pillar of 'SHAME' that once felt indelible.

'What is this if not spiritual?' I asked myself.

Let's return to the beginning.

My first word was 'light', according to Mummy. Before she pointed out the bags under my eyes, before she pointed out if my skin was clear or spotty, Mummy had been the first person to point me towards the light.

My inner child, my mixed-race butterfly boy, fluttered in the golden light. Not a godforsaken fallen angel but a butterfly aching to beat his wings, to follow his instincts, to do what makes him happy.

'Good boy.'

Effeminate boy.

'Will I ever get a boyfriend?'

Seven-year-old boy branded from head to toe with the Nike logo.

Boy who wanted to wear dresses, a crown of daisies and play with Barbies.

An abundance of other mixed-race boys around me.

The innocence I'd lost was returned to me. He grew towards love until he was light. Until he filled me completely. Until he wore my golden-brown skin snugly.

He was me and I was him. His hands were my hands rubbing my crown. My cropped hair was his cropped hair, but there was no Nike tick to be found there.

I looked down, he looked down. His eyes my eyes. With the index finger of my left hand, he poked my pot belly. He chuckled my chuckle. He smiled my smile. He put his left hand to his heart, and my heart raced for him, for Yiayia and Bapou too.

I looked up, he looked up. We saw my aunt and Theía clearing the kitchen table, a wordless act of service without expectation. We saw Theío sat directly across from me smiling without expectation. There was no more conversation. No more words of affirmation needed. Theío had told me, three times, he was proud of me. That was plenty.

'Páme, let's go,' said my aunt.

'Goodbye, Theía.' I stood and I hugged her.

She hugged me tightly and I could've rested my chin on her head.

'Goodbye, Theío.' I hugged him.

His hug was strong and sturdy and, as always, he kissed me on both cheeks. A perfect goodbye.

Recommendations

Books

Abraham, Amelia. *Queer Intentions: A (Personal) Journey Through LGBTQ+ Culture*. London: Picador, 2020.

Alabanza, Travis. *None of the Above: Reflections on Life Beyond the Binary*. Edinburgh: Canongate Books, 2023.

Amstell, Simon. *HELP*. London: Vintage, 2019.

Chapman, Gary. *The 5 Love Languages: The Secret to Love Thats Lasts* Chicago: Moody Publishers, 2015.

Dabiri, Emma. *Disobedient Bodies: Reclaim Your Unruly Beauty*. London: Wellcome Collection, 2023.

Dabiri, Emma. *Don't Touch My Hair*. London: Penguin, 2020.

Febos, Melissa. *Body Work: The Radical Power of Personal Narrative*. Manchester: Manchester University Press, 2022.

Gay, Roxane. *Hunger: A Memoir of (My) Body*. London: Corsair, 2018.

Gibran, Kahlil. *The Prophet*. London: Macmillan, 2016.

Haig, Matt. *Reasons to Stay Alive*. Edinburgh: Canongate Books, 2015.

Hewitt, Seán. *All Down Darkness Wide: A Memoir*. London: Vintage, 2023.

Hirsch, Afua. *Brit(ish): On Race, Identity and Belonging*. London: Vintage, 2018.

Hirsch, Afua. *Decolonising My Body: A Radical Exploration of Rituals & Beauty*. London: Square Peg, 2023.

hooks, bell. *All About Love*. New York: William Morrow Paperbacks, 2016.

Irby, Samantha. *Wow, No Thank You*. London: Faber & Faber, 2020.

Johnson, George M. *All Boys Aren't Blue*. London: Penguin, 2021.

Kolk, Bessel van der. *The Body Keeps the Score: Mind, Brain and Body in the Transformation of Trauma*. London: Penguin, 2015.

London, Iggy (editor). *Mandem*. London: Jacaranda Books, 2023.

Miller, Kei. *Things I Have Withheld*. Edinburgh: Canongate Books, 2021.

Patel, Shailja. *Migritude*. Los Angeles: Kaya Press, 2010.

Rosen, Michael (with drawings by Quentin Blake). *On the Move: Poems about Migration*. London: Walker, 2022.

Rothschild, Babette. *8 Keys to Safe Trauma Recovery: Take-charge Strategies to Empower Your Healing*. New York: W. W. Norton & Co., 2010.

Sheldrake, Merlin. *Entangled Life: How Fungi Make Our Worlds*. London: Bodley Head, 2023.

Sissay, Lemn. *My Name Is Why*. Edinburgh: Canongate Books, 2020.

Taylor, Joelle. *C+nto & Othered Poems*. London: The Westbourne Press, 2021.

Taylor, Sonya Renee. *The Body Is Not an Apology: The Power of Radical Self-Love*. Oakland: Berrett-Koehler Publishers, 2021.

Tsui, Bonnie. *Why We Swim*. London: Rider, 2021.

Wojnarowicz, David. *Close to the Knives: A Memoir of Disintegration*. Edinburgh: Canongate Canons, 2017.

Podcasts

Busy Being Black: busybeingblack.com

Gay Men Going Deeper: Apple Podcasts

Manatomy with Danny Wallace & Phil Hilton: Apple Podcasts

Mixed Up with Emma Slade Edmondson and Nicole
  Ocran: mixedup.co.uk
On Being with Krista Tippett: onbeing.org/series/podcast
Talk Easy with Sam Fragoso: talkeasypod.com
Where Should We Begin? with Esther Perel: estherperel.com/podcast
Word of Mouth with Michael Rosen: BBC Radio 4
Unlocking Us with Brené Brown: brenebrown.com/podcast-
  show/unlocking-us/

Support

NHS
For information and advice on health conditions,
  symptoms, healthy living, medicines and how to get help
Call for free 111
nhs.uk

Samaritans
For anyone who's struggling to cope
Call for free 116 123
samaritans.org

Stonewall
LGBTQ+ rights charity
Email info@stonewall.org.uk
stonewall.org.uk

SurvivorsUK
For male and non-binary survivors of sexual violence
survivorsuk.org

Switchboard
National LGBTQIA+ support line
Call for free 0800 0119 100
switchboard.lgbt

Acknowledgements

Thanks to Aissetou N'gom; Ajamu X; Alice Hiller; Alvin Carpio; Alycia Pirmohamed and the Scottish BPOC Writers Network; the American Library Association (ALA), the Chartered Institute of Library and Information Professionals (CILIP), and all librarians everywhere; Amy Zamarripa Solis and Writing Our Legacy; Amyra León; Andreas, Gabby, and the LGBTQ+ Cypriot Diaspora Group; Andrew McMillan; Annetta Benzar; Antosh Wojcik; Becky Thomas; Ben Connors; Benjamin Zephaniah; Bernardine Evaristo; Breanna McDaniel; Charlie Dark and Run Dem Crew; Cliff Joannou and *Attitude*; Damian Barr; Daniel Gorman, English PEN, and Scottish PEN; David Turner; Dean Krechevsky and St Mary's Hospital, London; Debris Stevenson and Mouthy Poets; Elizabeth Riddell and LGBT Health and Wellbeing; Eric Ngalle Charles; Farah Zeeshan and the Queer Writer's Circle; Faye Fadayomi; Gary Trowsdale, the Damilola Taylor Trust, and Spirit of London Awards; Hannah Gordon; James Mackenzie-Blackman and everyone I worked with at Lyric Hammersmith; Janet Iqbal; Jess Orr and Outriders Europe; Jim, Uli, and Erica at Gay's the Word, and every bookseller and bookshop everywhere; Joanna Lumley; Joelle Taylor; Johanna Clarke and the Society of Authors; John Agard; Kai Spellmeier; Kat François; Keith Jarrett; Kostya Tsolakis; Kris Black; Kuchenga Shenjé;

Lemn Sissay; Leo Metcalf; Lesley Wood and New Writing South; Lisa Mead and Apples and Snakes; Livia Kojo Alour; Maisie Lawrence; Malika Booker and Malika's Poetry Kitchen; Malorie Blackman; Matt Beavers; Matthew Xia; Michael Pedersen; Michael Rosen; Michael Twaits and The Art of Drag; Mónica Parle, National Poetry Day, and Forward Arts Foundation; Nafsika Atta; Niall Moorjani; Nii Ayikwei Parkes and flipped eye publishing for being the first to publish my writing in 2009, and everyone who has published me since; Nikita Gill; Nola Poltorak and ELOP – East London Out Project; Octavia Bright; Paige Ockendon and Metal Culture; Patrice Lawrence; Patrick Dunsmore; Paul 'Shez' Sherreard and Keats House Poets Forum; Paul Burston, Polari Literary Salon and Polari Prize; Peter Kahn and the Spoken Word Educators Programme; Peter Tatchell; Phyll Opoku-Gyimah and UK Black Pride; Ralph Hutton; Ruth Harrison and Spread the Word; Sabrina Mahfouz and Point Blank Poets; Salena Godden; Sam Morris; Shabnam Shabazi; Sharmaine, Symeon, Nels, and the Black Writers' Guild; Steven Camden (Polarbear) and the Roundhouse Poetry Collective; Stiven Skyrah; Sue Sanders, Schools Out, and LGBT+ History Month; Sunny Singh and the Jhalak Prize; Thomas Sammut; Tim Robertson; Tita, Maisie, Lindsay, and Glasgow Children's Writers Group; Topher Campbell; Travis Alabanza; Yiayia and Bapou; Zoe, Ari, Andi, and all my family.

'An Ode to my Black Queer Body' was first published in *Attitude*, March 2020, The Body Issue.

I wrote the 'Roots' section of this book during a trip to Greece and Cyprus as part of Outriders Europe, supported through The Platforms for Creative Excellence (PlaCE) programme, funded by the Scottish Government, the City of Edinburgh Council, and the Edinburgh Festivals and supported and administered by Creative Scotland.

With thanks to:

Publisher at Large	Francis Bickmore
Head of Editorial Management	Vicki Rutherford
Managing Editor	Leila Cruickshank
Editorial Assistant	Melissa Tombere
Copy Editor	Emma Hargrave
Proofreader	Alison Rae
Typesetter	Palimpsest Book Production
Communications Director	Anna Frame
Deputy Marketing Director	Caitriona Horne
Senior Designer	Gill Heeley
Rights and Contracts Director	Jess Neale
Senior Rights Manager	Charlie Tooke
Rights Executive	Phyllis Armstrong
Production and Metadata Controller	Hannah Watson
Sales Director	Joanna Lord
Head of UK Sales	Sasha Cox
Senior International Sales Executive	Rebecca Scott
Audio and Digital Manager	Gaia Poggiogalli
Publisher	Jenny Fry
CEO	Jamie Byng